Praise for *Strong Connecti*

"Mobile/cell-phone technology has an unparalleled capacity for bri the nearly one billion unbanked women into the formal financia tem. Rosa Wang has been on the frontlines of ensuring that low-inco women gain equal access to this life-changing technology and, with the full range of digital financial services. In her book *Strong Connections*, she tells the inspiring stories of the women who are working to guarantee equality of opportunity for women—as a path out of poverty and toward empowerment."

—Mary Ellen Iskenderian, CEO, Women's World Banking

"We all own mobile phones and know extreme poverty is real, but phones and poverty seem to belong to different universes. Wang takes us to meet those in extreme poverty, often illiterate, often without electricity or running water, and predominantly women, whose lives are being changed by their mobile phones (apparently more common in India than toothbrushes). It is an illuminating and often heartening journey."

—Professor Eldar Shafir, Co-author of *Scarcity*

"An engaging and inspiring journey through history, technology, and social progress from the frontlines of one of the most positive innovations (largely) improving life for many of the poorest people on our planet."

—Matthew Bishop, Author of *Philanthrocapitalism*
and Former Business Editor, *The Economist*

ɣ *Connections*, Rosa Wang provides endearing, enlightening, and dispatches from the front lines of the mobile phone revolution. -opening journey of opportunity and wonder."

—Roger Thurow, Author of *Enough* and *The First 1000 Days*

en we talk about increasing financial inclusion through the use logy, we talk about the technology itself or the potential impact mic growth. Told from the viewpoint of one of the veterans in d, *Strong Connections* provides real-world stories from people the r has met through her work in the field of what it actually means e financially excluded, and how technology-based financial products l services can change the lives of people—especially women—who live thout access to reliable electricity, water and sanitation, and education."

—Charu Adesnik, Executive Director, Cisco Foundation

"This is one of those rare books that takes you on a journey you didn't know you needed to take—and leaves you richer for it. With her gentle, unassuming style, Rosa Wang brings us with her as she walks alongside poor women (mostly) in Asia and Africa whose lives are being transformed by a small chunk of plastic and metal that so many of us take for granted. As we explore together, Rosa shares glimpses of ordinary women whose access to hope and a way out of poverty is grounded in the mobile phone revolution—and how their gender often slows that access. Never voyeuristic, she weaves these tales with glimpses of her own journey from high-flying financier to NGO advocate for digital finance, bringing the most practical solutions and building connections that are transforming our worlds."

—Robin Gorna, Writer, Activist and Founder, Women4Global Fund

Strong Connectio

Stories of Resilience from the Far Reaches of the Mobile Phone Revolution

Rosa Wang

Published by River Grove Books
Austin, TX
www.rivergrovebooks.com

Distributed by River Grove Books

Design and composition by Greenleaf Book Group and Mimi Bark
Cover design by Greenleaf Book Group and Mimi Bark
Cover images used under license from ©Shutterstock.com/Photographer RM; ©Shutterstock.com/Stanisic Vladimir

Publisher's Cataloging-in-Publication data is available.

Print ISBN: 978-1-63299-482-0

eBook ISBN: 978-1-63299-483-7

First Edition

for Priya

whose silence helped me

to find my voice

Contents

Author's Note

Most of the scenes in this book were reconstructed after I sifted through my own primary source materials: spiral-bound notebooks filled with handwritten notes, copious emails, and formal trip reports, as well as informal photographs, usually taken on my iPhone. Chapter 7 also leverages the notes and observations from my colleagues Nick Meakin and Dana Lunberry, and chapter 8 includes notes and observations from my colleague Sadhana Pandey. Some of the dialogue in both of these chapters was relayed to me in later discussions. In a few cases, timelines have been compressed so that events and conversations that actually took place over a couple of days are depicted as occurring on the same day.

Pseudonyms are used for some of the persons in the narrative. When someone is introduced with two names, such as Amolo Ng'weno, this is their real name. If they are introduced with one name, like Ruchi, this is a pseudonym. Except for Neema, the Tanzanian woman described in chapter 1, who is a composite of several persons, each name represents a single individual. Much of the dialogue in the book was conducted in the local language and filtered through colleagues who served as translators. I have tried my best to capture the essential meaning, emotions, and intent. I hope that all of the people represented in the book will find their portrayals acceptable. Any errors or omissions are mine.

Nalanda, Bihar, India, October 2018

Prologue

To Change Someone's Life

It is late in the day and the sweltering, humid air engulfs us. I'm with a team from a local microfinance network, and we are winding our way to our third stop of the day, this time near Nalanda, a town in the state of Bihar, India. We are driving farther north, deeper into a rural area, to visit our last agent of the day. The journey carries us over multilane, well-paved roads, then over a single-lane road with potholes, and finally onto a muddy, unpaved surface that slows our progress to a bone-jiggling crawl.

As we approach the market area, I see mostly boarded-up buildings and discarded metal car parts with rusty edges. A brown dog, one of the area's ubiquitous feral dogs, is dozing in the sunshine, and the few pedestrians tiptoe over him to not disrupt his canine slumber. Although we are not too far from Patna, the capital city of Bihar, it seems that we've stepped back to a sleepier time.

The intense late-day sun hits my face, and the humid air wafts over me. I instinctively reach for my water bottle, but then hesitate and put it back. While I should be thinking about the questions to ask the mobile-banking agent—a person acting as a human ATM, whom we are here to observe—it is hard to dismiss thoughts of how nice it would be to have a toilet break.

One of the unglamorous features of visiting the field means that there are stints of 10 to 12 hours when there are no toilet facilities available. Unlike my male colleagues, who can casually relieve themselves behind a tree, as the only woman in our group, I decide to spare myself the embarrassment and wait it out. Despite ambitious government plans to change, India still has areas where around two-thirds of families do not have sanitation facilities (such as a latrine). The lack of sanitation and clean water contributes to diarrheal diseases, stunted growth, and other challenges. I know that my discomfort will be temporary, and I will have access to proper toilet facilities soon, but for women and girls living in these areas, the lack of hygiene facilities has a huge impact on their lives. Girls drop out of school at puberty, women suffer from chronic infections, and infant girls often experience serious illness. I realize that my comfort is a trivial issue compared to the problems that exist here, but I also find it annoying that the organizers of the trip—all male, and all under the age of 40—probably forgot to take into account that I, a middle-aged woman, would be present.

Bihar is one of the areas in the world that scores lowest on human indicators like sanitation and clean water. There are complex, intertwined challenges that people face when living in poverty, but I am not here to work on sanitation or nutrition issues or to address the lack of rural electrification with solar panels. I am here with a team from our local financial service partner, to see if we can leapfrog technological roadblocks to help people, and especially impoverished women, adopt the mobile phones or some other form of mobile technology to do their banking.

Encounter with an Agent of Change

At 7:00 p.m., we continue our journey toward a market halfway between Patna and Nalanda. Suddenly the car swerves sharply right, dodging metal debris on the right side of the road while an errant motorcycle zooms past on our left. The papers in my lap go flying as I instinctively grab the seat in front of me to brace myself.

"Oh my God," mutters Akhil, our host and the supervisor of the banking agent program with Opportunity International's (OI's) local partner on the ground. "Does the motorcyclist have a death wish?"

"Tell the driver to slow down," says Vijay Singh Aditya, one of my associates. "We wouldn't want to damage the image of the positive things we've seen today."

Vijay unfastens his seatbelt to assist me in picking up the papers, but I motion for him to stay buckled up.

"The papers can wait," I say quietly, feeling the fatigue of the cumulative days on this trip. Privately, I wonder why they have scheduled this visit today, especially with a male agent, since we are in Bihar to monitor the success of the local agency's recruitment of women as agents. What more is there to see?

As we pile out of the car, Akhil tries to convince me that this is one of the best agents we are to visit. "You will see," he says. "Max is a very good agent."

Vijay also exits the car. I have known Vijay for nearly two decades. We met before I took on my current job, when he was named an Ashoka fellow, awarded by the world's largest network of social entrepreneurs. Vijay became a fellow in recognition for his entrepreneurial company that develops technology applications that serve the poor. As a technophile and champion of rural issues myself, I rely on his local knowledge and insights to push past the normal glossy message that foreign visitors to India are often given.

Our group, which includes several members of Akhil's team, trudges past the few remaining vendors, who seem to have sold out of most of their goods. I don't see the piles of stacked vegetables or rows of hanging garments that would be typical of a market like this. The pungent scent of fermented goat's blood hits my nostrils. There must be a butcher nearby. We then walk around several muddy patches, an indicator of the flooding that hit this area during monsoon season. When we arrive at the agent's shop, there is a large step up to enter.

Akhil tells us this agent, the cousin of the bank's loan supervisor, can speak a bit of English, so I can ask him questions directly. His name is Madesh, but everyone calls him Max, as he slightly resembles a particular Bollywood star.

As we enter the shop, Akhil says that the woman and man who have just walked in want to open a bank account. I was unable to observe this kind of account-opening transaction earlier in our visit and hope I will finally get to witness it in real time. We scurry in, and I ask Vijay and Akhil to step back and let Max continue without any interference or prompting so that the transaction will unfold naturally. If the attempt fails, I am interested in learning *how* it fails. I love trips to the field and ask that the visit be un-staged—that is, not have any formal structure or presentation—because that allows me to get a candid sense of what is going on, spontaneous and unvarnished. It's in remote areas like this that some of the best practices have arisen, bringing fresh ideas to my organization and its goal of extending financial services and training to unserved populations.

The woman is dressed in a simple sari with a maroon top. She has light yellow fabric hanging loosely on her head, and her hair is pulled back. Peeking out under the scarf, a mark of red dye rests on the part in her hair as if someone splashed it with ink. She is accompanied by a man wearing an orange polo shirt. The woman, whose name is Priya, has a rather sullen look on her face, and I remember that Vijay told me there were relatively few smiles in Nalanda. In her hand Priya carries a plastic shopping bag that lies flat, as if it might hold only a few sheets of paper.

The dot of red paint on her scalp indicates that she is married. The man accompanying her tells Vijay that he is not a relative but is simply there to help Priya and has escorted her from her village. It is likely that he is better educated than she is and is present to make sure she isn't cheated or assaulted. His presence also likely signals that her husband is not literate either. This practice of having someone with roots in the village help out is something I've seen in many states in India. Priya may have waited weeks or months until this man, a capable and trusted acquaintance, could accompany her to Max's location.

Priya and her companion approach Max, and the man in the polo shirt proceeds to do all of the talking. He indicates that Priya is in need of a bank account. She reaches into the plastic shopping bag and pulls out her Aadhaar national ID card and hands it to Max. (Aadhaar is a biometric-based identity system that India uses.) I don't want our presence to disrupt the transaction, so Vijay asks Priya and the man accompanying her if they would be willing to talk to us after they finish. The man agrees.

When I hear that Priya is here to open a bank account and is accompanied by a non-relative, my thoughts go immediately to what her circumstances must be like. On the surface, from what I can see, she and I could be quite similar. We seem to be of similar age (I just observed my 50th birthday) and are of similar height and build. Among commonalities that Priya and I likely share is a general sense of being mostly invisible. We are both mostly ignored by the men until our host informs them that I am the lead person on this project.

I also think of the many differences of our lives: Priya did not have the chance to go to school, whereas I spent over 16 years in classrooms and occasionally think of furthering my education. She doesn't have a purse but has placed some things in a small shopping bag, which might have been given to her by a neighbor. But mostly while looking at her, I think about the autonomy that I have experienced throughout my life. I had the ability to choose my major in college, to choose to leave my investment banking career, to work in places like this, to choose my husband.

Max pulls out a small biometric reader and motions for Priya to approach the desk. I pause and catch myself feeling a surge of energy. If all goes well, Priya will open a digital bank account and gain all of its associated benefits. I warn myself to keep my emotions in check, but moments like this are why I have been on this quest for over 16 years. Having a woman about to take the first step in gaining some financial control over her life is why I am in places like the outskirts of Nalanda, Bihar. I am optimistic that if things proceed according to plan, I can change someone's life.

Where Digital Progress Meets Reality

The story of the mobile phone and digital technologies is a very recent chapter in human history and innovation. Although most people recognize that their mobile phones are important and have changed significant portions of their day-to-day lives, many of us are unaware of just how deep and pervasive the impacts of the technology are. Still fewer of us in developed countries (or in the developed parts of our countries) stop to consider the challenges of reaching the people who are still on the wrong side of the digital divide.

Recently, I was speaking with a group of people far removed from those isolated places, who asked me how to better understand the lives of the people I had encountered, like Priya. I asked this group to try as much as possible to picture themselves in those same circumstances or, put another way, to walk a mile in the bare feet of those struggling in the developing world:

> Imagine what your life would be like if you never had the chance to go to school, had never learned to read. You wouldn't own books or a computer.

> You would see people walking around—people with more education, more resources—staring at glowing devices they called "smart." You would realize that those people lived in a world that was closed to you. Now imagine that you lived in a place with no electricity and no running water. The ability to complete household chores, like washing up, would depend on the rising and setting of the sun. A drink to quench your thirst could lead to diarrhea or fever. Words like Wi-Fi and internet would be outside your vocabulary. All of your meager savings might be the few pieces of metal that you wore on your body. Think of your anguish if you had to sell a piece to feed your children or pay their school fees.

This context is important because, despite progress in recent decades, those scenarios are the daily reality of hundreds of millions of the global poor in sub-Saharan Africa and South Asia. And persons living in conditions like this also represent the frontline of the mobile and digital revolution, the boundary where change is taking place, where phones and digital services are being introduced and opening up an array of possibilities previously unavailable.

It's with an understanding of the lives of those unlike ourselves that we begin to see why the story of digital banking is so remarkable. A couple of decades ago, if asked what the most common tool was for people around the globe, including very low-income people and those in non-electrified areas, most of us would have looked for a simple device, such as a hand tool or a farm tool. Some might have thought of a bicycle. And yet, as of last year there were about 5.5 billion owners of mobile phones and only 1.5 billion bicycle owners.

The Journey of This Book

It's been close to two decades since I left the high-octane world of investment banking, a career that I had pursued in financial capitals like New York and Hong Kong. Gone are the days of flying business class and staying in fancy hotels. My travels now take me to some of the poorest areas of the world. My current title is the global director of digital financial services for Opportunity International, which is a large network of microfinance groups that extend small-scale loans to very low-income people. To friends I describe myself as an accidental technologist, someone pushing for the adoption of the mobile phone and other digitally enabled services for low-income people, while not having a background in technology.

This book describes my journey of learning how culture impacts the use of technology. From joining raucous community center meetings with smallholder farmers in remote parts of Tanzania to sitting on the dirt floor alongside groups of non-literate women in rural India, the stories here chronicle the exponential trajectory of the mobile phone over the past two decades. These stories are woven through the arc of my own journey, that of an Asian American woman from Mississippi navigating male-dominated environments and cultures and changing the digital world.

Throughout this book you'll see that what started for me as common threads around technology and gender bias has progressed in the last few years to a near-obsessive quest to close the digital divide and to see how far the mobile revolution can be pushed in the pursuit of improving the lives of women around the globe. This is, to me, the last frontier of the mobile/digital revolution.

While much has been written about breakthrough technologies and early adopters who live where roads are good and smart devices are affordable, *Strong Connections* explores the largely undocumented journey of how mobile phones are entering the lives of those in extreme poverty: people, often women, often illiterate, who live without electricity or running water. I will tell you the rest of Priya's story and those of many other remarkable people—especially, but not exclusively, women—I've met in remote places.

I want to take you along with me on first-person trips to this last frontier. As part of this journey, we'll examine the creative ways that challenges—technological, environmental, and social—have been overcome. We'll probe paradoxes that occur when dealing with the uneven and intermittent spread of economic development. And we will investigate the details of how life has changed for many people as technology continues to progress. For future generations of innovators, there are lessons of how transformative revolutions happen on the ground, lessons that can be applied in other circumstances and scenarios.

Above all, I want you to explore with me the challenges that come with life on less than two dollars a day, and how in that world, the transformative power of digital technologies can give one an identity, improve one's finances, and bring some degree of empowerment to those who currently have none.

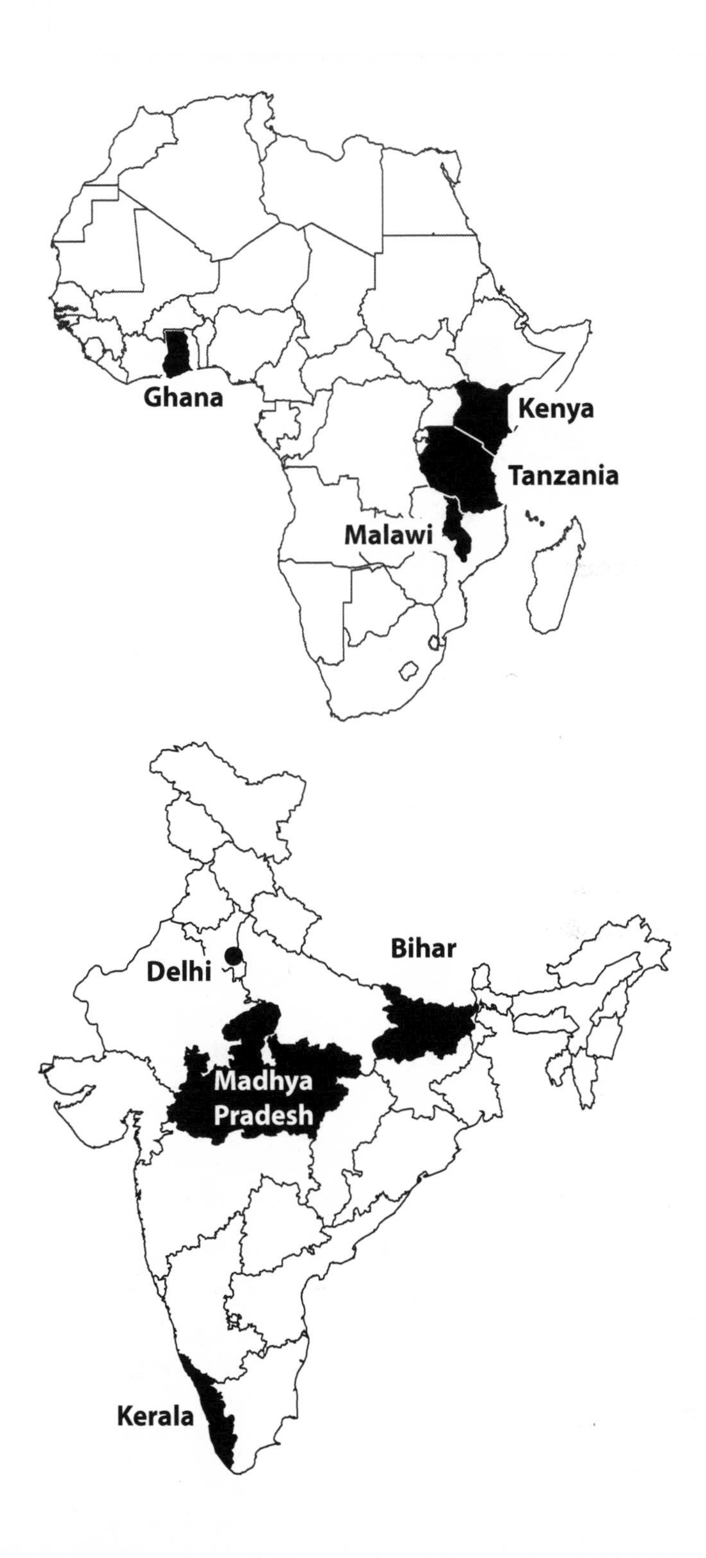
Ghana
Kenya
Tanzania
Malawi
Bihar
Delhi
Madhya
Pradesh
Kerala

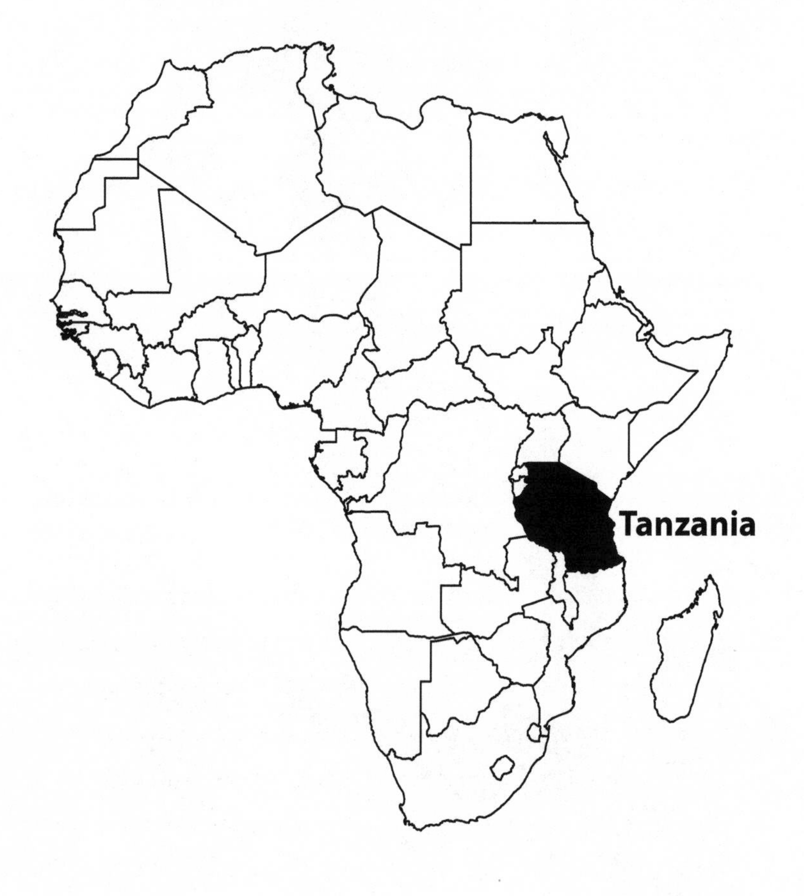

Dar es Salaam, Tanzania, Present Day

Chapter 1

How Far We've Come

The juxtaposition of a sophisticated digital device in a very low-income village can be jarring. Take, for example, Neema, a 34-year-old Tanzanian woman. She is representative of many East African women living across many countries in the region. Neema lives on the outskirts of the capital city of Dar es Salaam, and although her daily activities are very different from mine, her access and use of technology strike me with their similarities to my own.

Neema wakes up at 5:00 a.m. to prepare for the day. While her three children are still sleeping, she will have time to prepare the items for her food stall. It is still dark outside, so she lights a kerosene lamp to begin the day's preparations. Neema is a small-scale entrepreneur who runs a food stall in a bustling marketplace selling *muhogo*, a spicy cassava snack. Encouraged by her two sisters, as she was always the best cook in the family, she started her food stall three years ago. Every day, there is a lot of work to be done before she can go to the market: hauling water from the pump outside and firing up the cookstove for her three pots, one for the cassava, one for the spicy tomato and chili sauce, and one for the breakfast porridge that everyone will eat before the three kids rush off to school.

Her oldest daughter, Gladness, is the next to wake and wanders sleepily into the kitchen, smelling the pungent scents of fried chilis. Neema's phone beeps. She set an alarm the night before to make sure she and Gladness could complete their daily preparations. Gladness asks her mom if she needs help preparing more sauces. Without refrigeration, any perishable items must be made daily. Neema asks Gladness to check the propane tanks outside and then to chop more onions. With the propane Neema is able to serve piping-hot snacks, which has helped her business nearly double. It involves careful management of the fuel and hot oil, but her sales and profits have been good. When Gladness tells her she has only one spare tank of propane, Neema takes out her mobile phone and sends a quick text to the salesman, indicating she will need to pick up more stock in the evening.

Once the onions are chopped and all ingredients are in containers to travel to the market, Neema goes to wake up her two younger children and asks them to quickly get ready and put on their school uniforms. She checks that all of the uniforms are properly worn and braids her younger daughter's hair. The children have their breakfast of porridge, and then they all head out for the day along with Neema, who is pushing her food cart, now full of fresh ingredients to serve hungry customers. The market is over 2 km (1.25 mi) away, and the path, although frequently used, is still mostly unpaved.

In the right pocket of her blue apron, Neema is carrying her own mobile phone. She carries it everywhere she goes and is extremely proud to show it to me later that day. She was able to save up enough to purchase her own phone (her husband has his own) over the course of a few months. The handset has a simple numeric keypad and is a basic (non-smart) phone. While her hand-sewn apron, made of rough cotton and softened by years of handwashing, resembles one her grandmother would have worn, the device in her pocket is quite sophisticated.

Dumbphones Can Be Smart Choices

The outside of Neema's device is made of a high-grade, scratch-resistant polymer compound. The screen is made of a substance specifically invented to prevent it from shattering into small shards. Inside the device are billions of transistors, each no bigger than a virus, that function to process electronic signals.

Because of the popularity of smartphones among people with higher incomes, the basic handset that Neema carries is sometimes derided as a "dumbphone." However, building on multiple generations of improved design, her state-of-the-art phone has quad-band capabilities, meaning the same handset can work across a range of countries that broadcast their mobile signals differently. And there are over 500 patents whose innovations and design features are embedded into the phone.

Importantly for Neema, this basic device has a relatively long battery life and is affordable. By contrast, the smartphone that I carry runs on a relatively short battery life. I need to charge it at least once per day, which I can do readily, as my home and workplace are electrified. Neema, unfortunately, lives in a non-electrified area and must go to a charging station when she needs to recharge the battery. But with careful use, Neema's basic phone can last about 14 days on a full charge.

Although Neema has never been farther than 100 miles away from her home, the phone in her pocket contains components manufactured in Asia, half a world away. Phones like hers are made inside factory clean rooms where visitors have to don bunny suits (protective sterile onesies with feet, hairnets, and masks) so that not even a speck of dust can disrupt the production process. A visitor to one of these manufacturers would likely notice an absence of people in the production area. Stamping, etching, and quality control are done mostly by automated robots. A typical factory that makes the information parts of Neema's phone would cost almost USD$10 billion to construct. The company that created Neema's phone made about 100 million handsets identical to hers last year.

Each time Neema makes a call, most frequently to speak with a family member or supplier, her phone communicates with a mast, a metal tower 50 feet high, that relays her message to other towers. Today there are around 240,000 masts across sub-Saharan Africa. There's a mast located near the marketplace where Neema's food stall is located, so she has the benefit of a strong signal. Throughout the day Neema makes and receives several calls and also receives several text messages. The widespread presence of masts in the area where Neema lives means she is rarely outside of a good signal zone. When the phone is turned on, it periodically communicates with the nearest mast, which registers her location, so her movements are geo-tracked even with her basic phone.

Inside her phone is a subscriber identity module card, or SIM card, smaller and thinner than a US dime. This PVC-rimmed smart card stores Neema's phone number and a four-digit personal identification number (PIN) that she uses to unlock her phone. It also stores the phone numbers that she's saved, including those for her husband, her two sisters, her best friend, and her suppliers.

Having arrived at the place to park her stall in the market, Neema receives a call from her younger sister Imani. They speak every day. For Neema's call to be completed successfully, a signal has to be relayed across multiple masts, as her sister lives in the north near Arusha, nearly 400 miles away. Her sister also uses a different mobile network operator and has a different type of phone from a different manufacturer. Underlying the physical infrastructure of the service are a series of complex cooperation agreements or standards that allow the signals to talk to each other. These standards also allow Neema's SIM card to work in her phone and Imani's SIM to work in her feature phone.

Imani tells her sister that her mobile provider is offering discounted minutes on a special promotion, something she might wish to consider. The competitive environment for mobile services in Tanzania has been good for Neema and Imani. Their respective mobile network operators consider each woman a valuable customer, and they aggressively compete with other operators for the women's customer loyalty.

In the late afternoon, Neema packs up her food cart and heads home. Sales were good today; she ran out of *muhogo* before closing time and received many compliments on her spicy chili-garlic dip. She calls her husband to ask him to pick up more propane tanks on his way home, saving her the extra trip and bus fare into town. She then tries to call her older sister, but the line is busy, so she leaves a voice mail.

The Unimaginable Reach of Mobile Technology

Imagine if the world were represented by 100 people.

- Roughly half would be female and half would be male.
- Only 9 would be over the age of 65.
- About 60 of those 100 people would be from South and East Asia, and 16 would be from Africa. Only 5 would come from North America.
- Because of heavy investments in early education, only 14 would not be able to read and write, but two-thirds of those illiterate people would be women or girls.
- Out of the 100, there would be 22 without adequate shelter, and 11 would be undernourished; 33 would lack access to proper sanitation facilities.
- Fewer than 16 would own their own car; 21 would own a bicycle, which they would use mostly for basic transportation.

- Perhaps surprisingly, given these statistics, 72 of the 100 would have their own mobile phone, with many of the 28 non-owners being children. A full 96 of the 100 would be in an area covered by a reasonable mobile signal.

The global impact of mobile phones is hard to overstate. They have fundamentally changed economies and the notion of global connectedness. The mobile industry contributes 4 percent to global economic growth and underpins the employment of an estimated 30 million people.

As has happened for millions of people around the globe, the mobile phone has changed the way I interact with almost every product and service in my life. It has also displaced many of my other devices. I no longer maintain a fixed-line phone, an alarm clock, or a kitchen timer. In addition, I check my phone for basic information, and for things like emails and weather, on a constant basis.

Many technologies, such as the automobile and jet plane, have transformed the way many of us live. What is remarkable about the mobile phone revolution is its penetration beyond wealthy countries and communities, reaching not just high-income consumer classes but also low-income populations. The extent of this revolution, to reach people at every income stratum, including many of the very poor, is unprecedented.

Given that mobile phone users include those who live in areas without electricity or clean drinking water, the reach of this technology is even more surprising. Consider this: There are more mobile phones in Uganda than there are light bulbs, and more mobile phone users in India than there are users of toothbrushes.

Small Device, Huge Impact

For Neema, in rural Tanzania, a smartphone is not yet practical or affordable given her income, which is modest by global standards. But having a simple basic phone has made a profound difference in her life. She carries it with her everywhere and uses the phone to stay in touch with family, to help with her business, and to manage her vibrant social network.

Before they all had mobile phones, Neema and her sisters were able to connect with each other and their cousins only a few times a year, usually around holidays, at births of babies, or at funerals. As Neema slips the small, simple phone into her apron pocket, she smiles, knowing that this tiny handheld device, smaller than a deck of cards and weighing under three ounces, allows her to speak with both sisters almost every day, strengthening their already close bonds. Having never made a call using a fixed line, or an early generation mobile device, she would find some of the early history of mobile phones and services quite surprising.

Neema is asked for her phone number everywhere she goes. She obtained a loan from her microfinance group to buy the equipment for her hot food stall. They use her phone number to text her updates and reminders on her phone. The health clinic also has her phone number and asked if she wanted to sign up for updates and reminders. As she was born without a birth certificate, and before a widespread national identification program in her country, Neema's phone number increasingly serves as a unique way to identify who she is. This is foundational to a more empowered future for Tanzanians like Neema.

For the hundreds of millions of people like Neema who live in low-income areas, often without electricity, the mobile phone has become an astounding example of technology allowing people to leapfrog directly to more advanced technology, skipping many early stages of development. Mobile technologies allow people like Neema, who has never owned a fixed-line phone, never made a call on a rotary dial, to leapfrog directly to a state-of-the-art tool and benefit from services that leverage her device. She and the other market stall vendors would laugh heartily at the thought of carrying a phone the size of a large brick that weighed two and a half pounds. In the course of human history, the mobile phone revolution is unprecedented in its depth and pervasiveness. This is a revolution still in progress and one in which East Africa plays a leading role.

Enormous Benefits Today; How Did We Get Here?

Mobile technology has brought several enormous benefits to Neema and millions of impoverished people like her: a small, affordable, portable, durable device that can last several weeks on a single battery charge; good access to mobile phone technology; wireless services suited to life in a very rural, largely undeveloped area; and functionalities that keep users connected with family and allow them to run a business and receive health information and financial services.

Getting to this point has not been a quick or direct route, as I discovered on my journey from investment banker to champion of digital technologies for the poorest people on the planet. I took the first steps on this journey in 2002.

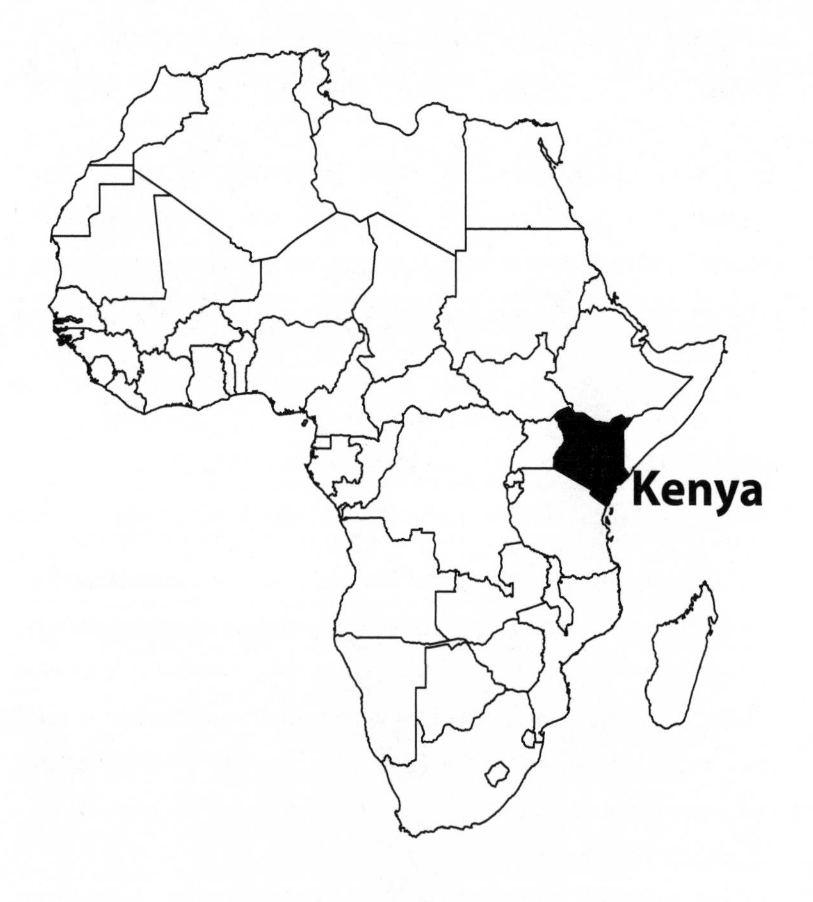

Maasai Mara, Kenya, April 2002

Chapter 2

Awakening to the Possibilities

I can remember the very instant when I really understood the difference that a mobile phone could make for a low-income person, especially for someone living in a more rural area. It was a light-bulb moment that would change my ambitions and life direction. Perhaps unsurprising in retrospect, my wake-up call took place in East Africa, specifically Kenya, later a key epicenter of mobile innovation. I was in the Maasai Mara National Reserve, a game reserve in southern Kenya. It was April 2002 . . .

On Safari

I drew in a long, deep breath as if I'd been underwater for too long and my lungs were starved for oxygen. Looking out, I could no longer see gleaming skyscrapers or hordes of fancily dressed pedestrians scurrying along the road, on sidewalks, and pouring out of buses and trolleys. Instead, all I saw was parched grass, a sea of light brown catching glints of gold in the late-afternoon sun, a lone acacia tree in the distance. I no longer heard the constant drone of a construction drill or traffic blaring, but rather the eerie quiet of near nothingness except for the noises inside our vehicle.

The sights and sounds were so different, each screaming out that I was no longer in the world that I had inhabited for seven years as an investment banker tethered to my trading screen. It was the simple act of breathing that underscored this point the most, reminding me that I wasn't in Hong Kong anymore. In that fast-paced Asian city, inhaling deeply seemed as if it should come with a health warning. I remember walking a few blocks in Causeway Bay, the corner of the island's industrial area, and nearly choking on exhaust fumes and black smoke. A number of people wore surgical masks when they ventured out, leaving visitors concerned about a plague or pandemic. But the air here, on this grassy infinite plain in eastern Africa, surprised me with its faint smell of hay and rain.

The Range Rover I was in lurched over the parched, uneven landscape. I was beginning to understand the benefit of the girdles created by Mongolian horseback riders that allowed them to avoid exhaustion after hours of having their innards juggled incessantly. Across the horizon, my untrained eyes saw almost nothing. I was looking at an endless plain with very little vegetation, a few lone acacia trees in the distance.

This was day 13 of an around-the-world trip structured around the location of my friends that was part travel, part escape, part discovery. In an uncharacteristically defiant fashion, I had quit my job in Hong Kong just a few weeks before without having a plan of what I might do next. I knew that the world of investment banking, despite being fast-paced, no longer held my interest.

Here on safari with my friend Amolo Ng'weno, who had been my roommate in graduate school; Amolo's four-year-old son, Oli; and our guide, Sam, Kenya seemed a million miles away from the world that I had inhabited just a couple of weeks prior. As I squinted through my sunglasses, I thought back to the gleaming office buildings, the endless team meetings, the constant wearing of a telephone headset so I could talk and type on my trading screen at the same time. Yes, Kenya was not just a different place but a different world.

"Over there." Sam pointed as he spoke, and we all looked where he directed us, though we only saw dry grass. "There, where the birds are flying. Rhino!"

Ahh, he was looking for motion and how it contrasted. Sam, the lines on his face indicating someone who must have been in his 50s, was the most experienced guide in the game reserve. He had found us a set of lionesses the day before. Amolo and I both noted that the younger guides would stop and ask to follow our vehicle so they could learn from Sam. He had accumulated years of experience in sighting big game and had enormous respect for the animals.

"Over there, the largest of the big five," Sam said.

"Sit down, Oli!" Amolo exclaimed more severely than usual. "Today would be a bad day to be eaten by a rhino."

Oli, with all the bravery of a four-year-old, started to sulk and then whimper as Amolo rubbed his shoulders soothingly. The night before, I was reading in a guidebook that four-year-olds are typically prohibited from joining safaris, as their size makes them easily mistaken for prey. Oblivious to the danger posed to Oli, I was focused on the animal ahead. A majestic black rhino, its large form accentuated against the sea of grass. Rhinos have been endangered, and we were lucky to be able to see such a grand animal. Sam had surpassed everyone's expectations.

"We should try to be very still," whispered Sam. "Rhinos will tend to ignore you if you stay out of scent range. But if they see movement, they could charge the vehicle."

Sam said this all matter-of-factly, but I didn't want to test the physics of a canvas-covered vehicle against an angry 2,000-pound wild beast. As with the lioness sightings the day before, as a city slicker seeing large animals in their natural environment for the first time, I knew I would remember the rhino vividly. It was the second most memorable thing that day.

Why a Rhino Came in Second

The most memorable event had occurred about an hour before. We were all loaded in the car, and Sam asked us how our night was. Amolo and I told him about the night safari we had gone on and how the teeming animals that used the cover of night to come out were in sharp contrast to the empty landscape that dominated the daytime.

Sam had pulled up to a Maasai man he called Olemeeli, walking along the path, dressed in full local costume. Sam started chatting with Olemeeli animatedly. I was studying his dress and the intricate beadwork that he wore around his neck, on his forehead, and on a really cool belt. Actually, it looked as if he had leaped out of my fourth-grade textbook. At that grade level we were studying different cultures, and our textbook included pictures of Maasai children.

Suddenly, Olemeeli placed his right hand into his brightly colored *shuka* garment. I shifted back for a moment. What was he reaching for? A spear? A stick? His hand swiftly pulled out a shiny silver handset that gleamed in the sunlight.

"Can I see that?" I asked, holding out my hand like a small child wanting to hold dad's tools. He held out the shiny object toward me.

"Just got this last week," said Olemeeli, obvious pride in his voice. "Everyone wants to have a look."

Before leaving Hong Kong, I had ventured to Mongkok on Kowloon Island, where every form of consumer electronic device could be found. Just for the trip, I had purchased one of the newer dual-band phones. Rare at the time, my new phone—which cost about three times that of my old handset—could be used in locations in Europe, Asia, and the Middle East, which were all on the GSM (global system for mobile communications) cooperative standard, plus in the US, where some of the networks were not part of the GSM. Though a bit heavy to carry, the dual-band handset had changed the nature of the trip.

Even though she wasn't traveling with me, I had been able to touch base with Amolo at all of my previous stops on my trip: in Dubai, at the Hong Kong airport, and at the resort in the south of Thailand that was five hours from the capital. Interestingly, I could get strong reception in Kenya, both in the capital of Nairobi and deep in the Maasai Mara National Reserve. The ability to stay in touch changed the way in which I planned (and worried) about the trip, providing an immediate pathway for learning about crucial flight change information and arranging last-minute logistics.

But back in 2002, mobile phones had not yet proliferated around the globe, and I was not expecting good connectivity in the game reserve. At the time, Nigeria—today Africa's largest market for mobile users—was still hampered by regulations that meant there were no commercially available masts to use with mobile technology.

Back in my previous life in Hong Kong, I had resented the incursion of the mobile phone. As one of the last in my social circle to purchase my own phone, I wanted to forestall the ability for my office to reach me all hours of the day and night, including weekends. I also recalled my then-employer's analysis of the expansion of mobile infrastructure, especially the recently held auctions for what was at that time considered the advanced 3G spectrum. Our internal equity analyst team, which had an excellent track record in picking stocks, thought that the companies bidding for the mobile licenses were overly optimistic. Just how many phones could a person have? How long would they spend with an attachment to their ear? Even texting, which then had to take place on a nine-digit keypad, seemed cumbersome and a bit alien to my fingers, which were used to a full keyboard. Surely, the dramatic forecasts for global adoption were overstated.

All of that changed the instant Olemeeli put his shiny new phone in my hand. First of all, I felt a pang of envy, as it looked nicer than mine. Being in this rural setting with a man in traditional costume, in a developing country that still had a large percentage of people in extreme poverty, made a memorable impression. It was then that I realized just how wrong I had been in thinking about the limits of mobile phone distribution. The ability for this technology to scale up, the demand for services outside of main urban centers, and the priority of investment by people like Olemeeli hit me all at once. Mobile technology may hold the key to closing a number of digital divides between the rich and poor, between males and females, between those in developed, urban areas and those in rural areas.

A New Path

After encountering mobile phones in the remote safari grounds of the Maasai Mara back in 2002, I knew that my assumptions about the digital revolution would need to be overhauled. I had a spine-tingling sense that I had glimpsed the future, and that this dynamic mobile arena might be something that I would find more captivating than investment banking.

What I did not know in 2002 was the deep transformation that would occur in the lives of people like Neema, the food seller of Tanzania, over the next decade and a half. Nor did I grasp how our journeys would one day cross. All I knew at the time was that I felt compelled toward something different, so I decided not to return to investment banking. Instead, I moved to Silicon Valley in California and immersed myself in the world of social entrepreneurship. For eight years, I worked with Ashoka, an organization founded to identify and support leading social entrepreneurs, remarkable people who were using entrepreneurial methods to address some of the world's biggest problems, like literacy, environmental issues, and maternal health. (This is the organization that made Vijay a fellow.)

Immersed in a sea of new ideas and exceptional individual achievement, I worked with entrepreneurs across all areas of social challenges and on various continents. A common thread emerged among those who had achieved scale, really large outreach: the use of mobile technologies. Infused with the restless dissatisfaction that has been a constant in my life, I began to wonder if working directly with communities serving the poor would be the best way to spread the mobile revolution.

As at many critical junctures in my life, there was a digital component. I had been recruited by my next and current employer, Opportunity International, through a social networking site as their head of Digital Financial Services. In this position I was to integrate the use of the mobile phone with the traditional financial services and training that OI had offered for nearly four decades. I would finally be able to integrate my business skills and social entrepreneurial knowledge to directly influence work on the ground. When I found out that the interview for the position was within walking distance of the house where my husband and I had relocated a year prior, the small English village of Oxford, I thought that fate had intervened.

But my first few weeks at OI were not as I had envisioned. Rather than being asked about my experience on projects in low-income communities, I ran into roadblocks. I was constantly overruled by men who had technology degrees and more years in traditional IT than I did, but who had minimal experience with low-income communities in Africa or India. A major point of departure was the desire to deploy smartphone-based financial services, something I thought was not well thought through given the lack of electricity and other challenging conditions of the clients we were trying to reach.

In fact, the work was so frustrating that I even wrote a letter of resignation, but fortunately before I could hand it in, I got the opportunity to leave that office in Oxford, England, and travel to remote places to meet and speak with clients. It was through those travels that I accumulated insights about what it would take for mobile technology to transform lives. Before I take you back into the field, however, it will help if you have a basic understanding of mobile technology.

Chapter 3

The Revolution to Date: Obstacles and Opportunities with Mobile Technology

Although the diverse functionalities available for mobile phones have entered virtually every element of modern life, the phone's history and exponential growth are as recent as they are surprising. The first telephone call took place in two adjacent rooms in March of 1876. Alexander Graham Bell uttered the famous line "Mr. Watson, come here—I want to see you" to his assistant, the electrical designer Tom Watson, completing a one-way voice call.

By October of that year, Bell and Watson had conducted the first two-way telephone call over a two-mile wire stretched between Cambridge and Boston, Massachusetts. It was the first wire conversation ever held. An audiologist who specialized in speech and elocution, Bell's work in telephony was intertwined with the development of the quality of voice sound. The telephone caught on quickly, and within 10 years Americans owned over 150,000 of the devices. In 1915, the first transcontinental call was made as Bell and Watson spoke over a 3,400-mile-long wire that connected New York and San Francisco.

A century later, the image of what a phone is and what it should do varies widely depending on whether you live in a part of the globe where roads are good, education is accessible to all children, and living standards are high or in a part of the globe where electricity and basic literacy are scarce commodities. Understanding these different environments is key to understanding how the mobile revolution has created both opportunities and obstacles for people living in underdeveloped regions of the world.

The Evolution of Form and Function

Since the early days of the telephone, there have been numerous attempts to remove the tethering of the devices to wires. The dependence on wires not only required both participants on the call to be at the specific location of a working phone but also caused calls to be bottlenecked by the capacity of that wire. In 1926, the German railway Deutsche Reinsbahn offered mobile telephony for those seated in first class, but service was limited to one route between Berlin and Hamburg.

In 1946, Americans tested a car telephone in Chicago, Illinois, that relied on radio waves that soon ran out of capacity. Just 10 years later, in 1956, the first phone for private cars was developed in Sweden. The phone resembled a large metal box with a rotary dial and weighed 88 lbs (39 kg).

In 1973, Motorola manufactured a prototype for the first handheld device, which weighed about 2.4 lbs (1 kg) and was about a foot long. This prototype was developed into the first commercialized model, the DynaTAC8000, in 1983. It had pushbuttons and an LED panel, weighed around 2 pounds, and cost USD$4,000 (more than USD$10,000 in today's money). The battery could last for about an hour, and 30 numbers could be stored in the phone. The bulky device seems massive by today's standards yet was the first step toward devices that would be carried everywhere.

At about the same time in the early 1980s, another development took place that would ultimately be important for the global scalability of mobile services—the ability of the devices and networks to handle increasing demand and make additional connections, including across national borders. Representatives from 11 European countries created a cooperative group known as the European Telecommunications Standards Institute that set the foundations for common standards and allowed for services that operated across national boundaries. In 1987, these standards were formalized as the global system for mobile communications, or GSM. (By the time Neema, the food vendor from the previous chapter, purchased her phone in Tanzania, the GSM was the standard for 193 countries and about 90 percent of the market.)

The GSM standards established in the mid- to late 1980s also covered the short message service (SMS), which allows 160-character messages to be transmitted on GSM mobile phones. But the first actual text message wasn't sent until 1992, when Nick Pappas, an employee of Vodafone in the UK, texted "Merry Christmas" to one of his colleagues during the company Christmas party.

By 2010, less than two decades later, an estimated 80 percent of mobile devices could send and receive SMS, and it quickly became employed in marketing strategies, first by mobile network operators (MNOs), then more broadly by companies for all types of goods and services. In that year, an estimated six trillion SMS messages were sent, and the global average price for the sender was USD$0.11 per message.

Although still popular, SMS as a portion of total messages has decreased in recent years with growing competition from mobile internet services and applications such as WhatsApp and WeChat. Particularly popular with younger users, the internet-based platforms do not have a per-message charge and can integrate additional multimedia features such as pictures, audio clips, and video. However, for users in many developing countries, where data connectivity is rare or very expensive, SMS still remains a popular choice. (Neema receives dozens of SMS messages each week.)

And it's not just texting that has evolved. In 1999, looking to go beyond the alpha-numeric SMS characters, the first emoji—or symbol represented as a picture, not letters or text—was sent in Japan. Over the next decade, the use of emojis would be very popular in Japan but would not gain large-scale traction in the US and Europe until standards were established. The adoption of emoticons by the Unicode Consortium—the group responsible for the standard coding of computer characters—resulted in uniform coding for emojis. These steps allowed for widespread use and recognition of the most used pictographs. In 2009, as part of the release of Unicode 6.0, there were 722 emojis. Eight years later, the Unicode list had grown to over 2,500 emojis, some globally widespread and recognized, and others used more within communities.

Basic Phone, Feature Phone, or Smartphone?

Today, there are three types of mobile phones available to consumers: basic phones, feature phones, and smartphones. I have owned and used all three types of phones.

In 1999, I purchased my first **basic** mobile phone, a small blue Nokia handset. It was an early model with a simple alpha-numeric keypad. I could make calls and receive brief texts.

In 2003, the first third-generation (3G) commercial services began to roll out, which allowed for the streaming of data. This marked the beginning of what is usually called *mobile internet.* The extension of 3G signals ushered in more advanced handsets that went beyond basic voice and text; these are known as **feature phones**. The additional functions of the feature phone might include a camera and simple games. Data and internet services were still very limited on this model of phone. (Wanting to upgrade my starter device, I bought a feature phone that year.)

Through much of the first decade of the 2000s, feature phones were very popular in the US as many users upgraded from their first basic phone to a more expensive feature phone. In Africa, feature phones have remained quite popular, bridging the gap between the constrained basic phone and the much more expensive, power-hungry smartphone. For example:

> Neema's best customer and friend Amos has a feature phone. Amos owns a shop on the north side of the market, where he sells paint and other household goods. His feature phone is bright red, has a much larger screen than a basic phone, and has a camera. But he likes it because it has a radio. He likes to listen to the political discussions and the play-by-play of global football (soccer) games. He is a popular customer at Neema's food stall because other customers know he will have the results of the previous night's matches.

The third category of devices are **smartphones**—devices that can perform a nearly unlimited number of functions via connections to the internet. Though smartphones didn't become widely available until the early 2000s, their history goes back a bit further than that. In 1994, when basic mobile phone handsets were in their infancy, IBM created what is considered a prototype for a smartphone, the Simon. To the extent that basic mobile phone development was driven by the desire for portability and scalability (the ability to make as many connections as possible), smartphone development has been driven by increased functionality, or the ability to add elements that one would find useful day-to-day. The first Simon had a calculator, calendar, address book, and touch screen, but it was not connected to the mobile internet as we know it today. Unfortunately, only 50,000 units sold. It had a clunky handset, but the main constraint was its battery, which lasted about one hour before needing to be recharged.

Through the early 2000s, smartphones were increasingly able to access mobile data. One of the biggest demands was for businesspeople to be able to send emails to colleagues while traveling, so buyers were mostly senior business executives in the wealthier markets. The BlackBerry by Research in Motion (RIM) became popular at this time and introduced a keyboard embedded on the device. The BlackBerry also had an instant-messaging service that allowed secure communication between two parties.

RIM remained the market leader through the mid-2000s, despite complaints of the keyboard's tiny keys. However, it began to lose that position when touch screens became more common. In 2007 and 2008, the iPhone and the first Android phones were launched, respectively, ushering in the growing use of smartphones (I didn't obtain my first smart handset until about three years later in 2011). Apple's first iPhone had a sophisticated operating system that, unlike earlier prototypes of the smartphone or feature phones, allowed for wider access and the use of internet broadcast by mobile, as well as connections to a wide range of sensors and support tools. In addition, Apple allowed the downloading of third-party software applications, or apps, that gave users access to externally developed functions. The first-generation iPhone cost USD$499 (for 4GB and USD$599 for 8GB) and had sales of 6.1 million units.

Continuous innovations have been made to smartphones, particularly to the software. Third-party providers have also created applications for the smartphone, contributing to rapid growth in the market and proliferation of functionality for each handset.

How Far and How Fast: The Push for Last-Mile Connectivity

The history of phone technology, and particularly mobile technology, has been shaped by the desire to bring connectivity to an expanding set of users. This is often described as **last-mile connectivity**, a term that initially referred to the set of technologies that bring the signal from the primary backbone to the consumer. This included telephones, traditional wiring, and fiber optics.

As services expanded, the term "last-mile" began to refer to the full set of solutions that would extend the service to areas previously uncovered. When mobile phones began penetrating into ever lower income groups, the communities of people represented were termed **"last-mile customers"** or users.

In developed economies, last-mile customers were often rural or rich customers needing to be enticed to add a mobile phone to their list of consumer electronics. In some cases, reaching the last-mile person meant convincing older customers, already equipped with and accustomed to fixed-line phones, that the benefits of mobile technology could outweigh additional costs.

In poor countries, the challenge was of course more complex, even though there was no competition from fixed-line services. Delivering services to last-mile customers became a buzz phrase among companies and entrepreneurs in the telecommunications industry. But unfortunately, when they said "last-mile" customers, they usually meant "next mile"—people just a little bit farther out from where services and technology were already available, not true "last-mile" customers, such as illiterate women or those in rural villages.

My own career has been shaped by the spread of mobile technology. When I first became interested in mobile phones in the mid-1990s, I still maintained (solely) a fixed-line number and never checked emails on weekends. At the time, I was living in Hong Kong, working in the world of investment banking and portfolio management. My team back then had placed a big bet on growth in the mobile industry. We held a higher percentage in technology and telecom stocks than our competitors and had thus outperformed them. As valuations and auctions of spectrum around the globe (the selling of the right to broadcast over certain bands of radio waves) continued to rise above expectations, we became even more immersed in learning about the industry and in routinely raising our forecasts.

One of the major views held widely across my investment team of 14, and supported by trips across the border into China each weekend, was a belief that demand from consumers in China was generally underestimated by investors in the West. We were confident this would be a major driver for the demand of handsets and mobile services with growth that could last years. Early demand for handsets by the Chinese surprised many of the consumer analysts. Rather than purchasing clunky, less-expensive handsets, the demand in China seemed to gravitate toward high-end, sleek handsets with a high price tag. The percentage of household income the Chinese would devote to a handset was substantially above conventional expectations.

My original concept of the addressable market, or forecasts of the ultimate reach of the technology, representing the potential for growth, extended to seeing mobile phones adopted by people living in Tier 2 cities in China (rapidly growing areas with at most a few million inhabitants). I did not think that mobile phones would deeply penetrate the developing world and reach remote rural populations.

That is perhaps why most people working with mobile technology, including me, underestimated its potential. Vodacom, the UK pioneer of mobile telephony, entered the market in the 1990s, forecasting that it would only sell about one million phones. Its UK-based competitor, owned by British Telecom, forecasted an addressable market of about half a million. Portability (remember early phones weighed about a kilogram, just over two pounds) and cost were big issues. For the first decade of service, most analysts did not see mobile phones as a mass-market product, thinking they would be reserved for the elite.

Those initial forecasts changed quickly. By 2004, in the UK, there were more active mobile phones than people. Now, smartphone usage has risen to more than half the market share of the total mobile market, and the percentage grows steadily. For mobile phone users in developed countries, where roads are good and access to the internet is comparatively more affordable, the smartphone has become integrated in almost all walks of life, displacing many standalone devices, creating a unified and portable access to streaming information. Increasingly, I use my smartphone to access financial services, health-related services, and music and video libraries, and as a way to maintain my social networks.

But with 250,000 patents embedded in today's smartphones, the cost of the handset and demands on battery power to run all of its functions still constrain adoption of smartphone technology in many developing countries. Yet even so, the extent to which technology has been integrated into the lives of people in even the remotest areas—and their ingenuity in finding the appropriate technology for their situations—has been a key insight for me and most other experts. My own understanding of all the factors that affect how technology is adopted, the barriers I thought would be in place versus those that actually were and the interplay of technology and social conditions, grew and changed with each visit I made to far-flung places.

Morogoro, Tanzania, February 2013

Chapter 4

Going Deep into Rural Territory: Testing the Limits of Mobile Reach

"Are you still coming?" shouts Emmanuel over the phone in an exasperated tone. "It's getting very late in the day."

"Yes, we're about 15 minutes away," replies Adrian Ghaui, our local facilitator, in a calm voice from the navigator's seat in our car.

"You said that half an hour ago!"

"Sorry, we made a wrong turn by the stream, had to circle back."

"As long as you are still coming." Emmanuel's voice is less shouty, more resigned. "The farmers are getting restless."

I am traveling with a team to visit farmers in hopes of seeing how far mobile technology has penetrated rural areas in Tanzania.

Emmanuel, the local organizer of the meeting, called us no less than four times in the past hour. At each instance, he sounded less confident about our arrival. Due to a lack of maps of the area and the unpaved roads, our journey has taken much longer than expected, and the group of about 60 farmers we are going to see has been waiting for nearly three hours before we finally step out of our cramped Range Rover and wander into the densely packed village meeting hall. Two meager ceiling fans attempt to move the humid, still air around without much success.

We can see the farmers—very few young adults, mostly middle-aged—shifting uncomfortably in the plastic chairs. They are dressed in jeans or coveralls, and several have on sports shirts bearing the logos of American basketball and football teams, the so-called dead-man's clothing that dominates Africa. (These previously used, donated garments often look as if no one has worn them, hence the name.) The few women farmers are dressed in long sleeves and floor-length skirts. One is nursing a baby; all are fanning themselves vigorously. There's a cacophony of voices, sort of like loud swarming bees.

Because of a miscommunication the day before, Emmanuel did not obtain chilled soft drinks, something that is typical for people to offer at community meetings. So not only are we late, but we are also bad hosts. We have also taken these farmers away from a morning of working in the fields, a high cost for people who tend small one- to three-acre plots as their main cash income. It is reaching the hot time of the day when the inland Tanzanian sun is directly overhead and there are no maritime breezes to cool us down, as happens on the coast. It is well past lunchtime, and the temperature is inching over 37°C (100°F).

Despite all of this, not one farmer has departed. Everyone remains waiting in the hot meeting hall because the topic of the day is something that could make a difference to their farming life: money. Specifically, we are here to talk about mobile money, meaning farm loans delivered not through a branch or a sack of cash but electronically by phone.

"The *mzungu* are here," I hear Emmanuel shout in Swahili, using the word for foreigner that dominates East Africa as we belatedly enter the meeting hall. Quickly, the voices and the bee-like sounds quiet down, and all of the farmers turn to stare at us as we take our seats in plastic chairs at the front of the room. I have an eerie, unsettled feeling as 60 pairs of eyeballs peer at me.

Is Branchless Banking Feasible Here?

Less than a week before, I received a call at my office in Oxford, England, from Cecil, Africa director for Opportunity International. I was still in my (frustrating) probationary period with OI, and he wanted to know if I would be available to get on a plane for Tanzania that Saturday. I had not informed Cecil that I was rethinking my new position, nor had I told him about a resignation letter I'd penned to my direct supervisor. I had left the office early one Friday not sure that I would return the following Monday. So the thought of actually going into the field, meeting real clients (the people we were serving), and seeing the situation and circumstances they lived in seemed like a good alternative to the office.

Cecil told me he'd like me to accompany my colleague John Magnay, a British agronomist and OI's head of agriculture. John, often regarded within OI as a bit of a maverick, had the idea that we could go inland and reach people farming small plots, usually of one to five acres. That meant we would not be visiting sites in either the capital city of Dar es Salaam (informally known as "Dar"), which sits on the Indian Ocean, or the northern inland city of Arusha, where OI had small microfinance operations.

Rather, we would travel to Morogoro, a town of 300,000 that lies within what had been termed the Southern Agricultural Growth Corridor of Tanzania (SAGCOT), a region that starts at Dar and runs inland all the way to the Zambian border on the west. This expanse, nearly 1,800 km across (more than 1,100 mi), dotted by towns along the way, had been designated as one of the development zones by the Tanzanian government and the World Economic Forum.

In typical understated British fashion, I could tell there was a subtext for my joining the trip. Cecil was hoping that I, with 13 years of commercial banking experience, would offer cautionary guidance and a risk management approach to temper John's innate enthusiasm.

"I want you to assess the feasibility of branchless banking," said Cecil.

Rural smallholder farmers represented one of the largest potential client pools for mobile banking. The prohibitively costly and labor-intensive model of brick-and-mortar structures that dominated urban microfinance were unsuitable in these rural areas. To be successful at helping rural farmers control their finances, we would need to use a digitally enabled approach.

But we couldn't rely on the same type of branchless banking that would become common in developed areas, where people simply used banking apps on their smartphones to establish accounts, make transfers, pay bills, and so on. In areas where smartphones and regular internet access were still a rarity, branchless banking often meant having human agents who could either provide the needed connectivity or assist people in using their own mobile phones to achieve connectivity.

"What do you mean by feasibility?" I put back to him.

"You know, the penetration of mobile phones, usage, ability to use phone banking."

"But Morogoro is really far inland, rural, and non-electrified," I said, knowing that incomes were much lower in these areas than in larger towns. "And isn't the urban pilot in Dar on mobile progressing a bit slowly?"

"Yup," said Cecil, conveying more than he intended.

I knew then that Cecil, and the broader team associated with risk and operations of OI, were hoping—or rather, counting on me—to come back with an assessment that illustrated we were in no way ready for a branchless pilot project, giving them a pass on internal tussles. There was a constant tension of trying to be innovative versus being too early. OI had a history of both substantial innovation and lots of failed or stopped pilots. Adding to a sense of urgency, we were working to a tight deadline, as we had to make a decision about whether or not we would kickstart a branchless banking program and get all of the internal systems in place and disburse loans in time for planting season. There were no relaxed bankers' hours or cycles in agricultural finance. The rains determined the timing of our activities.

"Don't expect too much," said Cecil, finally. "This is deep into rural areas. Many of the clients won't have phones." He paused for an uncomfortably long beat. "This isn't Kenya, is it?"

Despite his skepticism, I was relieved to have a chance to go into the field, to actually meet farmers. Compared to the past two months of frustrating office time, going to a rural agricultural community, where most farm families' yearly earnings were below the level of extreme poverty, sounded like a tonic. I immediately started packing.

Technology Aids Successful Farming

John, a farmer who has been based in Kampala, Uganda, for over 30 years, kicks off the discussion and introduces himself.

"Tell me about the crops you farm," he says to the group.

Kelvin, a short farmer from the second row, isn't shy. "I plant beans, tomatoes, rice, and maize," he says. These are ubiquitous crops that are well suited to the soil and water conditions in the SAGCOT.

"Tomatoes," chimes in Zacharia, a farmer wearing a thick plaid shirt and yellow hat. "They are in season now."

Tomatoes can be spotted everywhere along the roads, stacked up in unsupported pyramids, three to four fruit high, so everyone who uses the road can see the red globes and might be tempted to purchase them. Tomatoes are used in all sorts of stews and are a topping for rice. They are quite cheap, less than a few cents per kilo (about 2.2 lbs) and about half the price of tomatoes in the capital of Dar. But it is a long journey from Morogoro to the capital, and the effort and cost of transporting the fragile tomatoes to the big city would mean that the farmer wouldn't receive much for his efforts.

"I'm interested in the crops you *sell*," John specifies. Our team isn't looking for opportunities related to subsistence farming but rather commercial farming, where the farmer would sell the crop for cash. There's substantial muttering and jostling.

"Aah, then it's rice," corrects Kelvin.

"Rain fed or irrigated?" asks John.

"Rice, irrigated, five acres," interjects Matthew from the back of the room. He is a 38-year-old farmer who grew up in Morogoro just a few miles from the meeting area. He is at least 10, and maybe 20, years younger than the other farmers in the room and represents the next generation of farming. He has completed his secondary education and spent several years working in the capital city of Dar before becoming one of the rare educated people to return home to take over the family farm, which he did four years ago.

"Irrigated rice, about 5.5 acres," Matthew repeats clearly and authoritatively in English instead of Swahili. John, Adrian, and I look up, and our eyes fixate on him. He is wearing jeans and a Chelsea first-division football (soccer) jersey and is seated on an elevated shelf in the back of the room so he can see everyone. Because Matthew is both whip smart and street smart, the other farmers look to him to negotiate when foreigners come calling, despite his relative youth. He speaks fluent English, Swahili, and a smattering of other local dialects.

In addition to growing irrigated rice to be sold commercially, Matthew raises a range of vegetables to supplement his family's diet. Before arriving at the community meeting, Matthew already had a full day inspecting his land to ensure things would be ready for planting in a few weeks' time. Matthew is worried that the rains could be delayed again this year, something that made him almost default on his small loan two crop cycles ago. He also had a meeting with some visiting agronomists who were using a demonstration plot to show farmers a new way that fertilizers might increase their yield. Before planting season, there are always numerous meetings, lots of trainings and demonstrations for new fertilizers, higher-yield seed, and better irrigation practices. Matthew attends all of these.

For Matthew, the key to better farming is in the technology. He has a motorized water pump to irrigate his fields, and he has attended every farm extension provider training session available. In his hand he cradles what looks like a new feature phone, on which he receives weather information and information from the extension providers. Matthew's obsession with new technologies to keep up with changing farm practices has been mirrored in countries that have undergone a revolution in agro-business. For example, New Zealand, which underwent an agriculture revolution in the 1970s, saw over 90 percent of farmers leave the profession soon afterward. But overwhelmingly, those in New Zealand who remain have a master's degree or a bachelor's degree in agronomy or other farm practices because the requirement of knowledge and how to use farming technologies has become paramount. Today, despite its small size, New Zealand is one of the top exporters of several agricultural products.

Although Matthew does not know the details of the New Zealand agricultural revolution, he is aware that the farm practices that are being brought increasingly to Africa are necessary for the farmers to survive. He also knows that technology will play a key role.

While John continues to ask questions, my thoughts drift back to our trip to Morogoro from Dar the day before. We were traveling through one of the largest areas of potentially cultivatable land remaining on the planet. If Africa wanted to feed its teeming population over the next few decades, this area would have to be turned into productive farmland. Across the globe, it is remarkable how little of the land remains uncultivated. Yet during the long car ride to Morogoro, I was struck by the sparseness. We saw a lot of land that had not been touched, and the planted fields had almost no people working them.

Although our travel for most of the way was on reasonably well-paved roads, we had to compete with tractors, motorbikes, and public buses teeming with passengers. All along the way, everyone whom I saw—some standing at the roadside, others huddled in groups, young, old, men, women—was talking on a mobile phone. Even the police, dressed in bright white, pointed nonfunctioning speed guns at inattentive drivers while their other hands held phones to their ears. If an alien were dropped into the scene, they would probably think that this was a group of "black rectangle worshippers." I also noticed that many people cradled their handsets all of the time, neither putting them down nor pocketing them, as was my own habit.

Flimsy Cards Enable Wider Access

Adrian shifts in his chair, reaching into his pockets to search for a pen to take notes. Three small pieces of paper, just a bit bigger than a matchbox, drop out of his pocket. They are the scratch cards issued by the mobile phone operators. As the name implies, these cards come with a unique number obscured by a wax coating that has to be scratched off, allowing the user to add more minutes to make more phone calls.

As I help gather up the scratch cards, I take one in my hand and realize how flimsy it is but also how important. Scratch cards represent two ways in which mobile phone ownership has become accessible and affordable for dozens of farmers who live in remote areas and for millions in the developing world.

One of the early adaptations that enabled poor people to use mobile services was the adoption of prepaid or pay-as-you-go (PAYGO) services. While most people in rich countries subscribe to their mobile phone services on a monthly basis (also referred to as postpaid or monthly plan), in developing countries most people are on a PAYGO system, purchasing scratch cards like the one in my hand. The cards give them a certain number of minutes that they pay for up front. And when they run out, they simply purchase another card.

The scratch cards are sold at hundreds of thousands of kiosks that also sell household goods, cold drinks, and other items. At the time, sales agents are ubiquitous, even in very remote places. With prepaid minutes, a low-income person can begin to receive mobile services without a credit check and avoid being locked into a cumbersome subscription or ongoing monthly charges, things they are often hesitant to do if they have unreliable income. With the PAYGO system, the entrepreneur with irregular income could also avoid the problem of unused minutes or wasted subscription fees.

In Tanzania back in 2013, 99 percent of users were on a PAYGO basis. In fact, as late as 2019, well over 90 percent of mobile phone users in Africa still operated on a prepaid basis, with less than 10 percent on a postpaid or subscription basis. Worldwide, the majority of subscribers operate on a prepaid or PAYGO basis. In America, in contrast, the majority of mobile phone users, about 60 percent, are monthly subscribers, and only 40 percent operate on a prepaid basis.

The second significance of the scratch card is the concept of **sachets**. Long touted by proponents of bottom-of-the-pyramid strategies, physical sachets are used by consumer product companies to access low-income households. Aspirational brands, with items such as laundry detergent, shampoo, and even chocolates, are placed in small individual-use packages called *sachets*—they resemble a condiment packet at a fast-food outlet. This one-time-use packaging and pricing allow a low-income person to purchase a single sachet, often as a gift. In one of his well-known books, economist and lead proponent C. K. Prahalad terms this practice "the fortune at the bottom of the pyramid." He points out that very low-income people often work irregular jobs and their access to money is not a reliable stream the way it is for more formally employed people who receive a regular paycheck. Sachets, which require little up-front investment, make aspirational products accessible, creating brand awareness and loyalty as the individuals' fortunes increase.

For the mobile phone, the sachet concept means that users can purchase a brand-new SIM card (a new phone number) with about 60 minutes of use for about USD$0.60 to USD$1.00. A scratch card with enough top-up minutes, which may last a couple of weeks, is priced at a relatively affordable USD$0.08, paving the way for users in remote very low-income places to purchase what they need when they have the cash. The demand for sachets has turned out far beyond any forecasts or expectations of those familiar mostly with postpaid subscriptions, and it continues to grow to present day.

The scratch cards are problematic, however, because they are small—about 2.5 cm by 5 cm (1 in by 2 in)—and are printed on flimsy paper. So they are hard to manipulate, removing the wax coating on the back is challenging, and the cards require the user to type a unique 11- to 14-digit code into their phone to get credit for the minutes. In addition, fraud and theft of scratch cards is rampant.

So, while scratch cards make a significant contribution to the initial rapid spread of mobile phones, the provider companies are keen to move beyond scratch cards and create ways that minutes can be prepaid and simply stored on the phone or with the phone number. Ultimately, storing the minutes on the phone or phone number would give rise to services that allow a user to purchase more minutes and invest more heavily in their phone, creating what would become a store of value.

Basic Phones and Feature Phones Make Inroads

As I hand the scratch cards to Adrian, John signals it is my turn to ask questions, so I move to the front of the room.

"Who owns a mobile phone?" Every hand goes up, as far as I can tell. My eyes widen. My previous expectations that mobile phone distribution would be extremely limited in rural areas may be wrong, or at least outdated. But I need to make sure the group isn't giving misleading answers thinking I want them to say yes.

"What kind of handset do you have?" I ask.

Several farmers extend their phones in my direction, and I inspect four or five of these and ask questions about them. Most have a very basic nine-digit keypad, sometimes referred to as a dumbphone. I see no smartphones, but many farmers have feature phones. (These intermediate phones do not require streaming data, which at the time was still quite expensive in most African countries.)

Several farmers have dual-SIM handsets, a device that allows two different operator cards to reside in the phone so you can switch to another number without opening the phone and manually switching the cards. Dual-SIM phones are popular because the MNOs in East Africa compete aggressively on price, then fall victim to the constant churn of users, who are keenly attuned to promotions and discounts and therefore will switch to another network, leaving a provider whenever they want. Many farmers describe their phones as a recent gift from their family.

Holding a brand-new feature phone in my hand that has radio, a service rarely seen on American or European phones, my thoughts once again go back to our trip yesterday. During the long drive, Adrian and I reviewed the state of connectivity, mobile money, and mobile literacy in Tanzania. Having grown up in the SAGCOT region in a town called Iringa, Adrian, accustomed to a lot of services that underperformed, was pleasantly surprised with the changes that had taken place in the past couple of years as three MNOs aggressively competed for market share. The three MNOs created a level of competition and cooperation that did not exist in countries where one operator dominated the market. In addition, these big three brought substantial investment capital.

Just a few years prior, connectivity was expected only in urban areas. While coverage was still imperfect during our trip to Morogoro, there were regions that we visited where reception was good. We met other groups who were conducting field work and found they often used a dongle or a small plug-in device (also known as a thumb drive), and reasonable-speed data streaming was available, allowing for the checking of emails or the uploading of files. Understanding what this could mean for the farmers, my head is spinning with the possibilities of actually running a branchless and cashless loan system.

Back at the community center, my head-spinning continues as one man holds up what he describes as a triple-SIM phone. With his calloused, worn hands, he extends a very shiny silver handset that I have not heard about or seen before. I walk over to get a closer look, and he hands me the phone. Interestingly, the shape and size remind me of a *Star Trek* communicator, like the model I put together in my youth. Uncommon or prohibited in the US and many European countries where number portability is permitted, this is my first ever view of a triple-SIM device. I often challenged people in developed countries and non-governmental organizations (NGOs) to expect to see sophisticated digital devices, even among low-income people who live deep in rural areas. However, this is the first time I've spotted a sophisticated piece of hardware that seems widely owned in rural Tanzania.

Matthew, who also has a triple-SIM phone, explains that he can insert SIM cards from all three MNOs—Vodacom, Tigo, and Airtel—at the same time and use the one with the best discounts and promotions at any given time. As with the dual-SIM handset, the triple-SIM allows him to maintain a number with each service without having to switch the provider's cards. The fierce competition among the service providers seems to benefit consumers like Matthew.

Social Connections Lead to More Digital Connections

As I walk to the right-hand corner of the room, an older woman seated in the front row holds up her shiny new phone for me to see. She is notable because out of the 60 to 65 farmers in the room, she is one of only a handful of women and by far looks the oldest (she is 58). She is dressed in a full-length apron that covers a loose-fitting long cotton dress. This outfit allows her to move freely in the fields yet protects her from the sun; her hair is covered in a bandana in the fashion of most of the women in this area.

She says her name is Leyla. She farms irrigated rice and owns a motorized water pump just like Matthew. She raises a wide range of other crops, such as tomatoes, beans, and maize. She became head of her farm after her husband's death four years ago. Leyla has three adult children and several nephews and nieces. Although none of these relatives currently live near her, one or more of the younger generations are regularly around to assist with farming tasks.

That morning, Leyla was up at 4:30 a.m., well before sunrise. She prepared porridge for breakfast and snacks for later, after weeding. Her nephew was home for the week, and she had two additional day laborers to help, and they would all be very hungry after a few hours in the fields. After she prepared breakfast, Leyla carefully saved the ashes from the fire. She would use these to treat certain kinds of blight, as the pH level of the ashes could counteract certain fungi. Leyla knew this, as it was knowledge passed down by her husband and her grandfather, who taught her about many ways to take care of delicate plants. Leyla didn't like the new kinds of fertilizer and pesticides that the extension workers brought—she found they made her hands, and the hands of her workers, swell up after distributing the chemicals in the field. Before arriving at the community meeting, she had already inspected the tomato crop, which would be ready for harvest in the next three days, and the area where rice was planted, the main cash crop of her farm.

At the meeting, she hands me her phone and indicates that this nice feature phone was a gift from her children. She uses it to call them regularly, but also to call the day laborers who help during planting and weeding. She also calls suppliers and wholesalers who will ultimately buy her harvested rice. And the younger farmer Matthew calls to encourage her to go to the extension trainings; she's attended many, but with more skepticism than Matthew.

As I inspect Leyla's phone, a deeper understanding of the investment that her whole family made starts to sink in. Part of the error in forecasting mobile phone penetration in low-income communities is a lack of understanding of their patterns of saving and often extensive social networks. In the case of Leyla, her family helped her accumulate the money to purchase a nice handset, for they saw it as an investment to help increase farm productivity and income.

This same calculation was made across millions of very low-income households. At the time, roughly half of adults around the world had their own mobile phone, penetrating not just urban areas but also areas outside of cities, rural areas, and farm communities. A key distinction to the success of the mobile phone, versus some other technologies like cookstoves or other household items, is that phones were viewed as a way not just to save a bit of money but also to earn more income; it could transform small business for people.

Leyla's phone demonstrates success in appropriate technologies. Several Ashoka fellows are working on myriad technologies for the poor. They described the challenge as turning need into demand. There are a lot of needs in rural East Africa, but a number of factors have to come together to create commercial demand. In the case of Leyla, she saw the future benefits of the phone for farm productivity, saved aggressively, and pooled money with her family members so she could invest in a phone that would work for her, thus fulfilling her business needs and living conditions. Her need for mobile services was turned into commercial demand when the phone was purchased. As of 2012, when I met Leyla, around 32 million new handsets were purchased across Africa on an annual basis, as more and more people rationalized the cost and investment for this valuable tool.

Mobile Money and Mobile Banking

We turn our attention from phones and connectivity to home in on the appetite and readiness for mobile money. The integration of mobile phone services that can send and receive money is critical for our branchless program to work. Prior to the introduction of mobile money, the lack of ease and lack of affordability in sending or receiving funds presented a major problem for rural economies across the world.

The day before, Adrian and I reviewed the current status of M-Pesa in Kenya, a service that links the mobile phone with the ability to send or receive money. Wildly successful, M-Pesa (the *m* stands for "mobile" and *pesa* means "money" in Swahili) is revolutionizing everyone's thinking and whetting their appetites for mobile-based services, which could tie into the all-important financial services.

Although mobile money started out with slower growth in Tanzania than in Kenya, 2012 seems to be an inflection point, as more and more Tanzanians become familiar with this form of financial service. Certainly, there is aggressive promotion of the service throughout the country. And the unique trio of competitors created a competitive market where fees are proportionally declining, and competition drives the providers to up their service quality.

At the community center, my biggest concern is that aggregate statistics often mask the significant urban-rural divide. While I expect reasonable availability of *wakala* (the human ATM agents) in urban areas and large towns, I am concerned that all of the signs we see of *wakala* in the area, sometimes four or five signs on a small wooden hut, do not signify an active agent where substantial business can be conducted.

"Who has been to a *wakala* recently?" I ask.

Mwamba, an older farmer dressed in a blue shirt and cap, raises his hand. "Yes, I was at the *wakala* yesterday."

"Tell me more. What did you do?"

"My son who works in Dar had sent money," says Mwamba. "I went to pick up my cash."

"Did the *wakala* have sufficient cash?"

"Yes, of course." Mwamba smiles. "Charles is a good agent."

"If Charles doesn't have enough cash all at once, he will get it for you the next day," offers Kelvin, the farmer seated next to Mwamba.

"Is Charles an M-Pesa agent or a Tigo agent?" I then ask, mentioning the two most popular forms of mobile money available in this area. I am trying to see which provider we might consider partnering with.

"It's Charles," Mwamba says.

"Charles is an agent for both," clarifies Matthew, continuing his role as farmer whisperer for us. "Sometimes my cousin sends me money for our grandma through M-Pesa. Sometimes through the others. He tends to use the one running a promotion."

The previous day, before leaving on our trip, I asked my contacts in Dar if they used mobile money. Everyone in the office confirmed they did. When I asked which provider they frequented the most, they gave me the address where the agent kiosk was located.

In the capital city, the MNOs would staff the kiosks that experienced a lot of foot traffic with different people, sending a substitute agent if the first one was sick. During busy times, such as the weeks before Christmas, when a lot of people are sending money to relatives, the MNOs might have the kiosk staffed with multiple employees. I recall a conversation that I had many years ago with Ashoka fellow Anshu Gupta, an expert on rural communities who made this point many times: Everything is different in rural areas—reference points, the passage of time, and the importance of human interactions. In the urban area, for the office workers in Dar, an agent corresponds to a fixed location. Here among the farmers, an agent is clearly a known person, a relationship, not a place or a kiosk. I make a note to explore this idea further later.

"Do you find this mobile money service expensive?" I ask.

"Not too bad," says Mwamba. "Charles deserves the fee, and the last was only a couple hundred shillings."

"Two hundred shillings?"

"That's for the second tier," clarifies Kelvin, who then proceeds to quote the entire fee structure, which is based on a sliding scale. The MNOs, although transparent about fees, have not simplified it, sticking with seven levels of charges. Adrian has a flyer with the fee structure in his notebook. He nods, confirming what Kelvin has memorized about the fee structure, a sure sign Adrian is an active user.

"Are you also familiar with mobile money and the *wakala*?" I ask, gesturing toward the other side of the room. All of the farmers I am looking at nod. The fog of exhaustion and disorientation of the day seems to dissipate. A growing feeling of exhilaration starts to take over.

I ask the farmers to raise their hands if they have used mobile money.

Eighty percent of the hands, including Leyla's, shoot up. John and Adrian look at me in collective surprise, and slowly both nod at me. We should be able to leverage the existing ecosystem, rather than build everything ourselves from scratch. This is one of the most important facets of the rapid spread of digital services. I also expect it to be controversial, especially among some African bankers more accustomed to owning and controlling things.

Raising Expectations

Here in 2013, it is 11 years after my eye-opening experience at Maasai Mara and my first encounter with an advanced mobile phone in an extremely remote area. I'm not too surprised that some forms of mobile technology have penetrated into undeveloped areas, but it amazes me how the majority of farmers in this group, many of whom had no formal education, are already using money services on the phone. I once again need to adjust my expectations upward.

John, Adrian, and I drive back to our hostel that evening and agree to meet up for dinner in an hour. After a long day of sweating, a cool shower and a cold beer will be very welcome. But first, I need to send an email to Cecil and break it to him that against his earlier expectations, I'm not going to give him excuses to stop the project here. On the contrary, the branchless pilot is a go. Mobile money has clearly reached rural Tanzania. I do not have false illusions about the tasks ahead, but suddenly the unlikely plans seem a little less out of reach. I can also put away the resignation letter.

Lilongwe, Malawi, December 2015

Chapter 5

Malawi Reminds Me of Mississippi: Mosquitoes and Red Dirt

A faint buzzing noise makes me sit bolt upright in bed. The air conditioner, already questionable, has stopped, leaving me in a pool of sweat. With no power in the room, the light on the back of my phone serves as illumination to inspect the mosquito net above me. All four corners remain tucked in, and I feel satisfied that I'm in a mosquito-free zone. Then, I attempt to resume sleeping in a pool of sweat, an exercise in futility.

This is Lilongwe, Malawi, a malarial zone I'm visiting for the third time in less than a year. The work is exciting but frustrating and seems very far from my home in Oxford, England. I recall my first trip here a few years ago; I had to look at a globe and Wikipedia to learn more about Malawi. Malawi is ranked 209th among countries by income, and most Malawians lack basic services. Almost all are farmers.

For the previous 13 years, I have been drawn to places like this and have led teams trying to bring solutions to the complex problems caused by extreme poverty. As always, I am not here to install solar panels or work on childhood nutrition but to introduce modern technologies, to further the adoption of the mobile cellphone. Our local partner on the ground is Opportunity International Bank of Malawi, known by its old acronym OIBM. With a cooperative executive team, OIBM shows signs of progress on developing digital customer services.

Mornings start early in Lilongwe. Taking advantage of the daylight, we head to the branch in Area 23, a section northeast of the city. The drive from the head office, located more centrally in town, takes longer than expected and crosses large sections of mud and potholes. The axles of the cars would appreciate a cooperative effort to smooth the road's surface, but that level of cooperation doesn't seem to exist.

I quiz my local partners on the state of the roads. "Why don't the merchants in this area get together and share the costs of paving the road?"

"They don't trust the others to pay their share," offers Victoria, head of the marketing department for OIBM. It seems a low-trust environment undercuts many infrastructure projects.

Having spent a week already in Malawi, one of the things that has struck me is how much more expensive things are here. Not just on an income-adjusted basis, but on an absolute basis. In addition to the faulty supply chains and difficulty transporting things from point to point, many different types of goods and services are expensive. When I went to pick up some forgotten toothpaste yesterday, I found basic toiletry items like soap and shampoo are broadly similar in price to what I would pay in the UK; my typical lunch of fish with rice and greens at a food kiosk frequented by locals is about 40 percent more than what I paid for similar items in Kampala, Uganda, just a few weeks prior. Incomes per capita in Malawi have always ranked as one of the lowest globally. One in four of its citizens live below the World Bank extreme poverty line, one of the highest ratios in the world.

Higher price tags also apply to mobile phones and digital services. The Department for International Development (DFID) of the UK ranked countries by the percentage of disposable income spent on mobile services. For rich countries, the percentages were relatively negligible, at most in the single-digit percentages. In South Africa and Kenya, two countries where mobile services are widespread, the percentage was about 5 percent. However, in Malawi, according to this survey, households spent over half of their reported income on mobile services, including calls and texts, one of the highest percentages in the world.

My first reaction was to dismiss the data, but as I have ongoing conversations with my contacts in Lilongwe, I've begun to appreciate the broader context of the poverty that exists here. On a previous visit, I instructed David, who headed up client training at OIBM, to experiment with the new mobile money system by Airtel (a system to send money from person to person). When I saw him the other day, I was eager for an update.

"Can you tell me how the mobile money experiment went?" I asked.

"Well . . ." A long pause, then, "Let's just say I don't wish to repeat that."

I pulled him into an empty office. "Please tell me what happened."

"At first I was enthusiastic when you told me about sending money to my relatives using the phone," David began. "So I went to the Airtel agent just around the block."

"Did you have any issues with this agent?"

"Not really." He then continued in bursts. "I had to retry the connection twice, but the agent offered to help. I sent money to my mother, like you suggested. Then I called to let her know and told her to go to the Airtel agent that is in the market near to where she stays."

I had a foreboding sense. "What happened with the agent . . . ?"

"She went," he said, "and the agent was someone she knew and was polite, but he didn't have enough cash to complete the transaction, told her to come back the next day." His voice quickened. "Then she returned the next day, and again he had insufficient cash, offered to cash out half of the amount." David seemed more resigned than angry. "Anyway, it took five days for her to finally receive all the funds."

"Did the agent . . . ?" I began, but David was already on to the next example.

"I also sent money to my aunt. She didn't go to school, you know, so I support her." He continued apace. "Then I sent money to my son, who is studying in Blantyre."

"I would expect he would have an easier time navigating the menus," I said. The overall situation was starting to make itself clear.

"My son had no difficulty with the phone part, but the agent asked for an extra, under-the-table fee."

This surprised me. "But that's illegal. The agent could be suspended for asking for more."

David shook his head. "You have to understand, this service is new here; the agent probably felt he deserved to be paid more than the stated commission rate."

As David continued to tell me the stories of the funds he attempted to send—to his adult children, to extended family, to a relative paying medical bills—the full realization that he is supporting around 10 adults enveloped me. This network of adult family members likely extends to over 20 people including children, all depending on his one non-corporate salary. I also realized that the fees charged for mobile services, while insignificant in rich countries, could signify that someone had to skip a meal to buy more minutes or to try to send money to a relative. I was finding it hard to breathe.

"I'm so sorry," I finally uttered. "I know I encouraged you to try this."

"You didn't know what would happen," he replied without any sense of blame. "But I don't plan on trying this again until I can see some big improvements have been made here in Malawi."

I asked David where I could find Michael, the staff person who was focusing on agents. I wanted to make sure he was fully aware of the textures of these experiences.

"Michael is in the hospital. He should probably be back tomorrow."

"Hospital? Did something happen?"

"He should be fine by tomorrow; it is probably a recurrence of malaria."

Are Low Expectations Self-Fulfilling?

We arrive at Area 23, a large open-air market to the north of town, where dozens and dozens of stallholders set up six days a week to sell their goods. My senses are heightened when I'm in the field. The sun seems brighter and hotter; colors are more saturated, like the maroon of painted storefronts or the lovely yellows and blues on women's clothing. Soft sounds, like a whisper or a mosquito buzzing, seem like a loud roar.

As I'm taken to new place after new place, I find that I'm constantly on alert with an extra dose of adrenaline. This causes my emotions to be heightened as well, and for them to seesaw dramatically. A small bit of unexpected good news brings a rush of elation, and, similarly, disappointing news or encountering further challenges feels like a plunge into the depths of despair. I remember telling my husband that I would trade some of the heights to avoid the deep troughs.

It is already very hot, and mosquitoes and flies swarm in the open-air market. The scent of freshly slaughtered goat is pungent in the air and intermingles with the smell of DEET insect repellent that I have coated myself with. We enter a darkened entryway that blocks out the scorching sun. The inside of the shop is illuminated by a single light bulb, and the shop attendant, a young woman named Elizabeth, helps customers and collects payment.

On a large table I see a car battery connected to what looks like a rat's nest of black cables. Squinting carefully, I can see that each cable is tethered to a simple black phone. I count 16 phones, basic handsets with numeric-only keypads, all of the same make and model, all black.

"All the phones look the same. How do you tell them apart?" I ask.

"Most people recognize their own phone easily," says Elizabeth. She gestures to the side of the third phone. "See the scratch here?" She turns over the seventh phone and shows a barely perceptible mark. "And that one has a different scratch there." She tells me that sometimes a customer will leave and come back quickly when they realize they have picked up the wrong phone.

A man called Moses, who is ready to leave, lingers over the cluster of phones. Moses turns over three phones to inspect their undersides before being satisfied he has selected his own.

"How are you sure that's yours?" I ask.

"I usually put mine on the left side, the top position," laughs Moses, "but today, someone was already using that slot."

In Malawi, an estimated four out of five OIBM customers lack electrical power in their main residence, raising the importance of charging stations. Each week or every other week, a trip to recharge the phone is part of a regular routine, making it possible to own and operate a mobile phone despite not having electricity at home. A phone with a long battery life becomes essential. A weekly or bi-weekly visit to the charging station is manageable, but a visit every day, or every four hours (the capacity of some of the lower-cost smartphones), is not. Back in my investment banking days, we had not considered that large communities of people living without electricity would end up investing in and purchasing a digital device. My own expectations of the use and spread of the technology continue to increase with every field visit in Africa.

We walk from one end of the market to the other, headed to the Area 23 branch of OIBM. The market paths are unpaved, so the red dirt forms a coating of rust-colored dust that gets all over shoes, white shirts, and hands. The dirt reminds me of my childhood in Mississippi, in the southeast of America, the US's poorest state. It's the same iron-laden sandy soil that is only suited for growing a few crops. The heat, humidity, and mosquitoes also remind me of Mississippi.

Thinking back about the weather and red dirt, I am reminded of another common thread, one that has always annoyed me. As we walk, the staff try to downgrade my expectations. For example, when we approach Elizabeth, one of the agents, they tell me not to expect too much because she doesn't have a good education. As we are walking through the marketplace and I see a merchant who could possibly become an agent, I'm told once again to expect very little. I used to hear this a lot growing up: Don't expect too much, and you won't be disappointed. Like my early days in Mississippi, the constant lowering of expectations here seems often self-fulfilling. I couldn't help feeling that if the staff had more confidence that their work might lead to success, this would translate to greater success on the ground.

• • •

The next morning, at just past 7:00 a.m., I have cleaned off the red dirt on my shoes, which took two scrubbings. I head to morning devotions, the regular start of the day for OIBM staff. As I scamper in, worried I might be late, the familiar sounds of a church choir are echoing with the words of the hymn "How Great Thou Art."

Worship, with songs in both English and Chichewa, comes next, and everyone bows their heads and voices their prayers simultaneously until an even louder voice unites us in group prayer. There is a brief devotion by someone from OIBM's legal team, preferring the King James version of the Bible: "Let a man so account of us, as of the ministers of Christ, and stewards of the mysteries of God" (1 Corinthians 4:1).

There are staff announcements and then final singing accompanied by dancing. I am transported back to my time in Southern Baptist churches in Meridian, Mississippi—not the usual church that I attended for many years, but the predominately African American church that I would visit if a friend was singing a solo or for a wedding. My colleague who gave the devotion has the same inspiring cadence as the African American ministers of my childhood, engaging the listeners in call and response. The hymns radiate with joy and movement.

I love devotions at OIBM. They underscore the purpose of the work, something that helps bring colleagues together. And in the face of very challenging work, I sometimes feel that this early morning gathering might be the only time during the whole day when I feel wholeheartedly good.

We are going to visit an agent in Area 25, which is about 15 minutes away from Area 23. We drive to somewhere outside of the city, passing fields of maize, the ubiquitous crop of Malawi. Area 25 is one of OIBM's busiest branches, and everyone speaks highly of the branch manager, Ruth, who is a top performer in all areas. OIBM's foray into branchless banking means it has recruited agents who conduct some financial transactions by phone away from the branch. As we turn off the tarmac onto open greenery, I see several new buildings that look like a few small sheds. From a distance they look ordinary, like the structures of my elementary school, very boxy with flat tops. Everything is painted in the OIBM's regulation maroon and white colors. Then I see that the building is made of recycled shipping containers.

Outside the building, there is a sun umbrella and chair where an agent, Chimemwe (which means "happiness" in the local language), is stationed to assist bank customers. She wears a cobalt-blue dress with a beautiful embroidery pattern of beaded swirls. Her hair is pulled up in a fashionable high bun. I feel underdressed. Over the gorgeous blue fabric, she wears an apron that says "Banki Mmanja" in the local language of Chichewa.

Banki Mmanja and the Invention of Mobile Money

Banki Mmanja (meaning "bank-in-your-hand" in Chichewa) is the term used by OIBM staff and customers to describe their agency banking business, which was created to be a local version of Kenya's now famous M-Pesa. Created in 2007 in Kenya, in less than a decade the M-Pesa had completely transformed the Kenyan economy and the global understanding of the possibilities of integrating the mobile phone and monetary services. Based on the idea of an electronic wallet (a virtual storage of money), the M-Pesa system was constructed so that a simple drop-down menu would allow the user to send money to another person; pay bills, such as those to utility companies; or just store it (meaning it could act like a savings account). It had the benefit of not needing a smartphone or internet connectivity, as the menus could be used on basic phones and without an internet connection, with sufficient information going over the same bandwidth as a normal voice call.

At the time, there were significant numbers of Kenyans migrating from rural villages to the capital city of Nairobi or the coastal cities like Mombasa to find work. With no access to formal financial services before M-Pesa, many Kenyans would pay upwards of 25 percent of a sum of money in order to engage an informal (and illegal) network to send a transfer of money to their relatives in the village. When Safaricom in Kenya set up the electronic wallets, they also trained a series of shopkeepers to work as agents, or points at which cash could be turned into electronic money that would be sent to a relative's phone number. Their relative, in the village, would find a local M-Pesa agent and be able to collect the funds as cash. In theory this transaction could be instantaneous. In practice, a whole series of correct steps would need to be in place. As initial traders began to use the service, investments were made by the parent company, Vodafone; the UK government arm DFID; and foundations, such as the Bill and Melinda Gates Foundation, to grow the service and extend it to the Kenyan population to improve economic development.

By 2016, M-Pesa in Kenya amounted to over 1.7 billion transactions. The user base represented over 90 percent of the adult population; the value of funds transacted was equivalent to 48 percent of the GDP and dwarfed the value of international remittances.

As the number of transactions on M-Pesa grew, so did transaction sizes. Originally promoted as an alternative for Kenyans who did not have access to formal bank services, upper-income Kenyans migrated to the service as well. M-Pesa could be used to purchase everything from a bus ticket on the local *matatus* (buses), worth a few cents, to an airplane ticket for an international flight, worth thousands of dollars. The easy access to mobile money had the effect not only of changing economic flows and releasing bottlenecks but also of making Kenya, and particularly Nairobi, a port-of-call for innovation in mobile services. I would spend a disproportionate amount of time in Kenya, bringing people from other countries to learn, meet other innovators, and take advantage of its new status as a mobile talent magnet and incubator.

As M-Pesa in Kenya proliferated and began to dominate the economy of Kenya and spread to other East African countries, many others tried to copy or create a similar service. The telecommunications company Airtel had launched Airtel Money in Malawi, but in the early days the lack of customer training and challenges with the agent networks meant that there were few users. OIBM, which had already linked bank accounts to the phone, decided to launch its own agents to try to address the void. Having so few people with experience in other parts of East Africa who had experience with a successful agent network turned out to be one of the biggest barriers to a faster launch in Malawi. While there were case studies about successful examples, there was a lack of experience and thus uninformed expectations around how to get the network on the right trajectory, which should have been toward significant growth.

Happiness Is a Successful Agent

Michael, the staffer who oversees agents for OIBM, has recovered from his bout of malaria and is accompanying me to Area 25 to see the woman sitting under the sun umbrella. He tells me her English is okay but tries to lower my expectations (I'm not surprised!). An interesting miscommunication led to her sitting just steps from the front door of the bank's branch office. I asked Michael to set up an agent "near" the branch—I had in mind half a kilometer (about three-tenths of a mile) or so. Michael interpreted "near" as "next to" the branch, which we later both found amusing. However, it turned out several customers were willing to use the agent and avoid the long lines that formed for branch service.

The woman enthusiastically offers a handshake and a broad smile. "My name is Chimemwe."

I encourage Chimemwe to tell me about herself. "Why did you want to become an agent?"

She says, "In school, I liked numbers. I had heard that there are jobs like accounting. So I decided I wanted to become an accountant and work in a bank." She takes a long pause before continuing, "My grades weren't good enough to study accountancy, so I dropped out of school."

Her face brightens as she tells me that now, as an agent, it feels almost like working in a bank. She finally gets to deal with numbers and money.

Chimemwe shows me her ledger from the day before. She completed 22 transactions, each for a commission, showing that she is one of the better performers among the new recruits.

"Are you happy with the number of transactions you're doing?" I ask.

Her reply is forceful. "Oh, of course." Even if she were not happy, she could not say this in front of Michael. I need to find another way to have her share more of her experiences.

"I'm really glad you like being an agent, but tell me how many transactions would make you really happy."

"Thirty," she states immediately, demonstrating that she's calculated the commissions she would receive. She is also considering the trade-off of her time and the cost of bus fare, lunch, and other factors. She shows me a handwritten notebook where she has noted each failed transaction and its cause.

"This is a very valuable journal. Can I purchase it from you?"

Michael looks at me with a bit of surprise. "She will probably give this to you."

"Possibly, but logging the problems is extremely informative. You want to send a message that the journal is valuable."

Michael and I discuss a fair amount of money to give Chimemwe, and I hand over some *kwacha.* I then urge him to contact the best five performing agents and tell them to keep a detailed logbook of failures, for which they will be compensated. Learning from failures is something that I hear every day, and yet,

I observe, most people shy away from speaking about failures and mostly talk about successes or about failures spun as successes. We need to encourage everyone to learn from mistakes, so we plan for a staff session to review the failure journals once they are collected.

We walk back to the front of the branch, where the bank tellers stand behind their respective counters. Ruth, the branch manager, now finished with her meeting, has joined us. I notice that a queue of over a dozen customers has formed, and I ask Michael if a member of the branch staff could encourage people to try out Chimemwe's service. Ruth, overhearing us, goes up to each person in line and informs them that an agent is sitting just outside. Customers are welcome to use her service, and there is no waiting there. Several of the women in line nod at Ruth but keep their places. Finally, a young man toward the back of the queue says he will try the agent and walks to find Chimemwe.

"Sorry." Ruth looks disappointed. "But I do think we can have a marketing officer offering to help tomorrow. Most of the women seem unsure of how to navigate the process with an agent."

"Don't worry," I say to her. "Everywhere in the world, including Kenya and Silicon Valley in the US, it's young, better-educated men who try out new digital services first."

Security and Safety for Women

I fill Ruth in on the failure ledger that Chimemwe has kept, and she immediately adds a few suggestions to improve the process. Having worked her way up from acting as a relationship officer in the field, she understands the customers, and I can see why she runs the most productive branch. As we begin to wind up our visit, I look at the women waiting in the queue.

"What percentage of these women have informed their husbands of their bank accounts?"

Ruth looks at me intently. "Not one. Absolutely zero." She continues, "You have to remember these accounts represent security and safety for these women. It is what they have to take care of their children should something bad happen."

I nod. "There is a story about the accounts here at OIBM that has become almost a legend, even overseas."

Ruth interrupts me with a big smile. "Ah, that story. It is true. The branch manager was my mentor."

"What story?" asks Michael.

Ruth tells him that three years ago, OIBM provided training for women, encouraging them to open savings accounts and informing them of their legal rights. Unlike some of the neighboring countries, a married woman in Malawi could open an account in her own name without needing her husband's permission. Legally, the account is hers. One day, a man walks into a branch outside of Lilongwe and demands that the teller hand over the contents of his sister-in-law's account. The branch manager is called and speaks to the man. When asked why he's there, the man says that his brother has just died, and he has heard rumors that his sister-in-law has an account at the bank.

The man states with confidence, "By our traditions, the contents of that account are now mine." That branch manager politely but forcefully asks the man if he has an account at the bank, to which he says, "No." Then the branch manager says he must ask him to leave and escorts him out because the branch only serves account holders.

Ruth smiles as she tells the important part of the story: *The next day, the queue of women to open accounts or to deposit more of their savings was triple the normal size.*

I then realize the critical issue that was staring me in the face while I was focused on infrastructure and financial spreadsheets: I need to focus specifically on the barriers that hold these women back. Their trust and confidence would be a force beyond any marketing budget imaginable.

Through word of mouth, the branch manager's actions—sticking up for the woman, a widow, against huge cultural pressures—became well known. In less than a decade, the savings base of OIBM swelled to 600,000 people, overwhelmingly women, and almost all of them very low-income. Locally, OIBM is known as the bank of the people, and increasingly, the people are served through their mobile phone or other digital channels.

Navigating Local Customs

Michael and I head back to the head office after our time in Area 25. We have a meeting with a group called e-Kwacha. They recruited Chimemwe and are willing to be responsible for the recruitment and training of up to 20 agents. In exchange they will receive a portion of the agents' commissions.

Michael needs to make a phone call, so I tell him I will greet the e-Kwacha representative first and he can join us in a bit. I race up three flights of stairs to the executive floor, where a young man, Ezra, is waiting in the hallway. Ezra is over six feet tall and looks as if he'd be a soccer player if he weren't working in financial services. I apologize for being late and point to an empty office where we can start the meeting. The room, used mostly for impromptu meetings, has the chairs to one side and desks in the corner. The Malawian afternoon sun has been streaming through the windows and the room is nearly 40°C (104°F). I fiddle with the remote for the air conditioner. Ezra stands near the door while I struggle with the remote. I finally get the air conditioner to start, and I notice he hasn't moved. I remember visits to Japan in my banker days when I could recognize there was some formality that I did not know about. I would wait for someone else to make the first move. After a long pause during which we are both standing motionless, staring at each other, Ezra walks toward the chairs.

"Ahh, I am not of this culture, so I can get my own chair," he says as he picks one up.

So many actions in Malawi that I did not fully understand, like the back and forth and giggling during the weekly staff brunch, now became clear. The women here are expected to serve the men, even in a modern office setting.

"Good idea," I say as I grab a chair. "Why don't we each get our own chairs?" Ezra is a Shona speaker from Zimbabwe, geographically not too far away, but culturally, his traditions are quite different.

I note with surprise that all of the agents Ezra has recruited have female names.

"Why have you recruited all women?" I ask him.

Ezra is confident this is the right direction. “We’ve been recruiting agents in Southern Africa for nearly two years. The women are more reliable. They focus on building their business, and there are fewer complaints.”

Thinking about our earlier interaction and how women are expected to take on serving roles, I ask, “Are there male customers that might not wish to go to a woman agent?”

“It’s okay. The women are there to provide a service.”

Expect More

In the late afternoon, the office people are starting to head home, and Michael brings me the summary sheet of the day’s transactions. He is excited.

“Chimemwe nearly made her target with 28 transactions today, a record high for her!”

I smile while scanning the data.

“Where is this agent based?” I point to the line corresponding to an agent who successfully completed 42 transactions in one day.

Michael examines the agent details. “This is Limbe, in the south.”

“Why is this agent so successful?”

Michael looks deep in thought. “I don’t know. I’ve never met him.”

He pauses, then looks up at me and says, “But I will go next week to visit and find out.” He smiles and adds, “He may be a good agent for the trainees to shadow.” Then, after a long interval of silence, “I really never thought it would be possible for an agent to complete more than 30 transactions a day.”

The teenage me, still brushing the red Mississippi dirt from my shoes, answers for the adult executive. "Sometimes it's good to expect more."

• • •

I walk back to the hotel. Although the sun has set, it's still over 38°C (over 100°F) and humid. After a long day, I'm ready for a shower and a tall, cool drink. I think about the progress made today and try to temper my expansive hopes with realism. Despite continuous challenges, I feel it's been a productive day, more so than most. As I enter my hotel room, I find a note under the door:

> Dear Valued Guest,
> Due to emergency maintenance, municipal water will be turned off for the next four days. Unfortunately, shower and bath services will not be available during this time.

Despite the minor inconveniences, this trip has been very valuable to my understanding of the state of mobile services. It is nearing the end of 2015, and mobile money has become ubiquitous across most of Africa, particularly East and Southern Africa. All telecom companies and many financial institutions have introduced their own version of banking by phone. More services are being offered, including insurance and connections to agriculture and health services. Women, while still lagging men in initial usage, are closing the gap in most markets, especially in Kenya. It is time for me to turn my attention to one of the largest markets in the world, India, where despite the widespread adoption of mobile phones, mobile money has yet to really catch on.

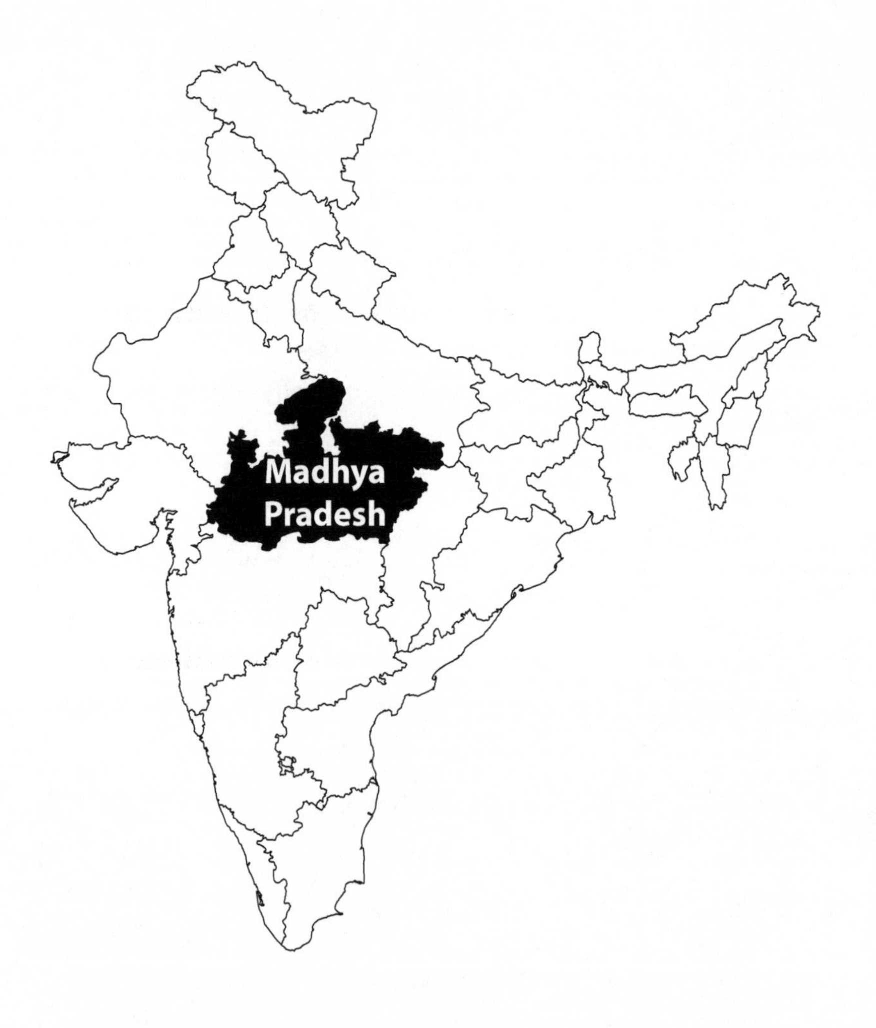

Bhopal, Madhya Pradesh, India, September 2016

Chapter 6

"Someone Has to Help Me": More Barriers for Women

It is only 8:00 a.m. and I'm already feeling the sweat trickle down my neck. Scattered clouds seem to enclose the area like a terrarium, and the air is thick and still. My childhood summers in Mississippi should have prepared me for this climate, but after several years of living in England, my blood has thickened. Fearing that my sleeveless shirt might seem immodest in this village outside of Bhopal, I keep my navy-blue suit jacket on. I am dressed for the chilly air-conditioned car that is standard for foreign visitors. I don't expect to be riding in a battered, oven-like Range Rover.

Half an hour outside the city, the driver pulls off the pavement onto a flat, barren plain, a place not of trees but of dust and scrub brush. After 20 minutes on bone-shaking, unpaved desolate terrain, the car rolls to a halt, and four of us climb out into the blinding white of the sun. We walk toward a tiny concrete hut, less than half the size of a small trailer home, that is covered with corrugated tin. The strong smell of manure hits our nostrils, the aroma from a lone water buffalo tied to the hut alongside a clothesline, where simple fabrics hang to dry. When I squint, I can see two similar huts on the horizon, but mostly I see an expanse of arid, uncultivated land. This seems an unlikely setting for the frontier of the digital revolution.

• • •

Bhopal is the third leg of this scouting trip in India. With my focus exclusively on Africa for the previous period, it has been over five years since I was last in India. During that time her population has grown by 77 million, equivalent to adding an entire UK or France. The place is now teeming with nearly 1.4 billion people, half under age 25. Overall economic growth statistics have told a positive story, with the GDP expanding by nearly 8 percent in the past few years, significantly outpacing the US and Europe and even rivaling Chinese growth rates. Mobile phone users in India have mushroomed to 685 million, more than double the entire population of the US. This is also year 14 in my quest to bring the benefits of mobile phone and digital services to those on the wrong side of the digital divide.

Seated on the Malwa Plateau in the center of India in the state of Madhya Pradesh, the city of Bhopal is known for its hills and two major lakes. It was founded in the 11th century and then declared a princely state in 1818. From 1819 to 1926, the area was controlled by four female rulers, which was unique for the time. They were known as the Nawab Begums of Bhopal. The state was the second largest Muslim state (after Hyderabad) in pre-independence India until it was merged with the Union of India and became administered by the Indian government in 1949.

Despite its interesting history, for most people, including me, the name Bhopal is synonymous with the disaster that took place in December 1984 when a Union Carbide India Limited (UCIL) plant leaked 32 tons of toxic gases, resulting in thousands of instant fatalities and dramatic footage of the suffering that took place being broadcast on television. In the disaster, the UCIL factory, a maker of pesticides, leaked the highly toxic substance methyl isocyanate gas, contaminating the air, groundwater, and soil in nearby small towns. Death toll estimates ranged from 3,800 to over 16,000, with a further 500,000 people believed to have suffered non-fatal injuries. The event is classed as the world's largest industrial disaster. The impact on soil and groundwater is still cited today, and health problems of community members persist.

To rebuild the Bhopal economy, the state government has invested heavily in higher education and attempts to encourage manufacturing of electronics. It has been declared one of India's 20 Smart Cities, part of an initiative to use data-driven methods for improved municipal services. Despite this heavy investment, Bhopal appears to be a quiet place not frequently visited by foreigners. Unlike the large jet planes that brought me to India, my transport to the Bhopal airport was on a small prop plane.

Despite the frustrations of my job, I am still enthusiastic about scouting trips because they are filled with potential and the excitement of seeing and learning about somewhere new. I find that I am often able to envision how technological and sociological changes I've seen over the past decade and a half might be transplanted to the new location and might grow and take off. My recent experiences in Africa, where mobile and agent-based branchless banking are expanding rapidly, are more relevant than examples from America or Europe and could have high applicability here. However, on this occasion my local Delhi-based partners do not share my enthusiasm. They point to the inequalities of development in their country, especially the challenges faced by rural women, and encourage me to temper my expectations. They choose not to accompany me on this visit.

Creating Trust

The four of us get out of the car, first the driver and I, then the chief operating officer (a young man in his 30s), and finally Praseeda Kunam, the founder and CEO of a small microfinance outfit called Samhita. She is a fearless Indian woman who left a comfortable executive job at a major European bank to turn her skills to a specialized area of small-scale lending. Samhita focuses on the extension of loans to women below the income levels of clients accepted by most other microfinance groups. Praseeda founded her organization about nine years ago and is one of the rare women CEOs in the industry. She will serve as my guide and translator for the day. So far I notice that Praseeda does most of the talking and occasionally asks the CEO a question.

We have arrived just in time for the group meeting already in progress. The four of us take off our shoes and enter the concrete hut through a thick woven blanket hung over a curtain rod. My ankle brace is now apparent, a concession to middle-aged aches and pains. Inside, the glare of the sun has been replaced by the light of a single naked bulb in a windowless room. This is one of the few electrified huts in this district.

I scan the room quickly. The center area has been cleared so the women can sit. They are called a *trust circle* or *trust group* because each member guarantees the loans for all of the members collectively. There is power in numbers. Against the wall, stacked all the way to the ceiling, are musty boxes, thick folded blankets, and what appear to be parts from used kitchen appliances. It reminds me of my parents' attic. Their own bouts of early poverty led to a lifelong habit of never throwing anything away. The storage area of my childhood home is crammed with cardboard boxes, slumping irregularly through age and re-use, plus broken blenders, toasters, and unmatched, chipped plates. However, in contrast to my parents' attic, in this hut I see no chairs, no table, and none of the numerous stacks of books or old magazines.

The group members, exclusively women, are a colorful contrast to the relatively drab surroundings. They are dressed in very bright solid colors; some are clad in all red, others in pink, and others in shades of purple. All of them have covered their hair in colorful scarves as both protection against the sun and as the custom of modesty in this area. Praseeda and I are the only women not wearing head coverings.

The meeting is already in progress. Fourteen women sit on the floor in two rows, their attention on one woman seated in the middle, Neva, the loan officer, who is one of Samhita's frontline staff members. She conducts these trust group meetings on a weekly basis, a time ostensibly to offer training and support but mostly to collect the weekly loan repayments. Wearing a green sari and orange scarf, Neva's henna-decorated hands hold a seven-inch Android tablet. Instead of green ledgers and manual receipt books, frontline field staff like Neva carry tablets outfitted with internally developed apps. Field operations require neither pen nor paper.

Neva calls out surnames in a clipped staccato and notes two absent women from the group. Absentees suggest stress in a household, and Neva will conduct roll call three times in the brief 30-minute meeting. If a woman arrives late or leaves early, this might warn of financial problems at home. The tablet assists loan officers and Samhita to create a digital footprint for the group members.

Praseeda moves to sit on the floor next to Neva and encourages the women to shift from their classroom-style rows to form a single circle so everyone can be seen. She pulls my hand and gestures for me to join the women on the floor in the now densely packed circle; my knees brush hers and those of one unnamed group member. A keen supporter of the empowerment that small-scale loans can bring, Praseeda is always trying to create an environment where the women will speak more openly. With a wave of her hand, she sends the two men who have accompanied us to wait outside. Now, with only women in the room, we are more likely to get candid answers.

The formalities of a trust group meeting continue. There are some half-hearted recitations of financial education lessons, but most of the attention focuses on the collection of that week's loan repayments. There's a flurry of discussion because the cash, counted out three times in quick succession by Neva in front of all of the group members, has come up short. I hear murmuring back and forth that gets louder and louder. Finally, one woman utters severely, "Ruchi, just give her the money. We'll settle later among ourselves." The oldest woman in the group reaches into the folds of her blouse and slowly pulls out a wrinkled 20-rupee note. If one woman is unable to pay on meeting day, the trust group rules require the others to make up the difference. From the rapid response of the women, I take it this happens regularly.

How Microloans Are Used

Finally, the business of the meeting being complete, I ask the women if they will stay to answer a few questions. Neva records the amounts of repayment on her tablet, says goodbye, and rushes to her next trust group. She will hold eight similar meetings today, servicing and collecting repayments from over 100 women. She has no time to linger.

"What did you use your loan for?" I begin, wanting to understand the financial state of the women. "Where did the proceeds go?"

I am peppered with a quick array of responses:

Jyoti, the woman clad in green, used the money to help buy a water buffalo, or *bhainsa*, as it's known in Hindi. She is able to sell most of the milk for a small amount of income.

Madhu works as a housemaid on an ad hoc basis in town. "I purchase cleaning supplies," she says. She hopes to earn more and build up her cleaning business.

Aditi, the woman in the pink headscarf, hesitates at first, then says, "I help to pay school fees." The loan supplements her husband's income and helps to keep her two children in school. Several other women echo the school-fee usage. They all have ambitions for their children to have easier lives than them.

Officially, the loans are intended to assist the women in creating small businesses or income-generating ideas, but Praseeda is pleased that these non-educated women are prioritizing the schooling of their kids.

Praseeda wants to hear more about how the loans impacted their lives. "What changes have you experienced?" she asks.

"We didn't think anyone would lend to us," says Madhu, as she tells us about the positive impact of having someone trust them enough to extend loans.

Jyoti is more specific. "My husband treats me better now that I am able to obtain funds for the household." Several other women indicate a similar kind of empowerment and respect at home since the loans have been obtained.

"I have been able to keep the kids in school," the woman to my right says in agreement as she taps my arm.

I next probe for the existence of formal bank accounts. Despite active promotion by the Reserve Bank of India for the creation of what they term no-frills accounts (accounts with no fees), use of such accounts here is nonexistent. I move to the next set of questions.

"Where do you keep your savings?" I ask.

Praseeda, who has been translating all the previous questions spontaneously, turns to me and whispers, "I don't think these women have much to save." She gives me a puzzled look, wondering if I have unreasonable expectations of the poverty levels here.

"Just ask," I whisper back. "I want to see *how* they respond."

"Where do you keep your savings?" Praseeda puts forward slowly.

Raising a finger to her chest, from the place she had removed the final 20-rupee note, Ruchi says, "Here."

Aditi, one of the younger women in the group, tells us she purchases gold. A common custom throughout South Asia, gold worn as jewelry often represents a woman's total emergency savings. Gold purchases are often a good barometer of economic growth in many areas. I observe that Aditi is only wearing a couple pieces of simple jewelry.

Pointing to the canister piled high above a stack of boxes, Jyoti says that she uses a similar container in her home to store any extra rupees. We collectively turn our heads to look at the canister wedged between boxes and blankets, pushed against the wall.

There are more hand gestures from a woman named Mena from the far side of the circle. She tells us that she splits the cash across multiple canisters and hiding spots.

"I used to bury money in the back garden," Madhu inserts, "but one time I forgot which spot it was buried in." She stifles a nervous giggle.

Several women speak at once, pointing at objects in the stack against the wall where money might be secreted away or talking about locations around their homes that might serve as a good hiding place. Soon all of the women are talking, making hand gestures and laughing. I stop scribbling on my notepad, realizing that it is the first laughter I have heard during this visit.

Chandni, one of the latecomers, joins in indicating she has also forgotten some of the locations of hidden cash. Her voice is a soft whisper.

Praseeda turns to me, one corner of her mouth turned up, a mix of bemusement and new understanding.

Social Barriers to Mobile Technology

Feeling that we have a better sense of the women's financial circumstances, we are ready to turn to the main point of my visit.

I start with the most basic question. "Do you have a mobile phone?"

I see two women raise their hands—hands that are worn and aged by years of work: laundering clothes, cleaning homes for the rich, tending to small garden plots—their calloused fingers cradling a simple, basic black handset.

I am not sure what I was expecting, but certainly more than two. Perhaps they misunderstood that I wanted to see their phones right then, so Praseeda asks individually if they have a phone, but all of the other women shake their heads no. Basic handsets are what I'm accustomed to seeing, but 2 out of 14 is disappointingly few. My heart sinks as the reality of the situation starts to sink in.

Connectivity is not the problem. Intense competition for India's growing mobile appetite means that numerous companies have spent billions on masts with strong signals to try to carve out a slice of the market. My iPhone is showing four full bars of reception, and Neva is able to use her tablet without interruption. I've been to areas that I thought were economically similar, both in Africa and in other states of India. In the previous locations phone access was higher, in some cases much higher. More worrying, programs like those I launched in Africa over the past three years would normally require at least half of the group members to own their own phones from the start. I take a deep breath.

"Is there a phone in your household?" I ask next.

All the women bob their heads in the Indian motion of assent.

"The phone belongs to my husband," offers Rani.

"Your husband's phone?" I say.

"Yes, husband's phone," affirm several in unison.

I look up from my notes and scan the faces in the group all staring back at me. My mood lifts slightly. In this group, at the household level, ownership of at least a basic handset is 100 percent. With around two-thirds of adults owning a mobile phone in the country, despite very low income levels, this group has above average household coverage. They have already surpassed one of the initial hurdles by accumulating savings to obtain a digital device. My growing realization is that mobile access is a priority here, *at least for the men.*

"Are you *allowed* to use it?" I choose my words carefully, trying to tease out any cultural barriers or insights about the factors that underpin this glaring gender gap.

"I don't know how," Aditi quietly replies, adjusting her pink headscarf. "Too hard."

Chandni and Jyoti tilt their heads in agreement.

Too hard. The words keep echoing louder and louder in my mind. I sit in silence, gathering my thoughts. Praseeda is also sitting quietly. Multiple threads race and jar through my head, colliding in a flurry of statistics, observations, and emotions. I just read a case study about the difficulty some South Asian women have with remembering a four-digit PIN. In that example, similar groups of women, lacking education and literacy and living each day bereft of things we take for granted—a calendar, a watch, a newspaper—never developed the specific mental skills needed to quickly memorize four random digits.

But that case study doesn't seem to fit this group of women. Though never formally educated, this group clearly has facility with numbers. They manage to access small-scale loans and, importantly, understand the value of trust and helping each other. For oral cultures around the world, mobile connectivity has unleashed massive pent-up demand to reconnect, especially with family far away. I need to probe to see if I am getting an inaccurate picture.

"Tell me. What do you do if you need to call your sister?" I finally ask, knowing that this activity would be common. As is the cultural custom in many parts of the subcontinent, young women are married off to men from outside villages and sent to live in unfamiliar households, surrounded by strangers. The phone call represents a last link to filial bonds. To call a sister would be an important, perhaps lifesaving part of being married. "How would you reach her?"

Ruchi looks at me with a steady gaze. "Someone has to help me."

A Long Way to Go

This visit to Bhopal has left me with a visceral understanding of the challenges faced when bringing mobile technology and banking to rural women. I wasn't inquiring about navigating a complex menu or new app; I was just asking these women if they could use a mobile phone to make a simple call. Without that ability and the confidence to try, household ownership and general connectivity won't matter much.

In the months prior to this trip, I was developing family training programs that would help husbands appreciate the potential benefits of having wives with digital skills and allow for the sharing of a costly device among several member users. But the challenges and compounded barriers faced by the members of this group are a step beyond anything I have previously addressed.

I feel a sense of sadness, as I have to admit that I have met other groups who had similar needs around technology and banking but who were more digitally ready to move forward. It might be a couple of years before there is something suitable to address the needs of these women in Bhopal. I can only hope that this is an exception and not the rule.

Patna, Bihar, India, November 2016

Chapter 7

Agents of Change: The Importance of Human Connection

Abhijit pulls up to a ramshackle storefront at the crack of dawn, the sunlight more lurking than shining. He carefully steers past two mud puddles, parks his motorcycle, and begins to open up his agent business. He plans to get a coffee later when the coffee vendor is open, because he had to wake early to feed the chickens and was up relatively late the night before teaching his adult literacy class. Abhijit is proud of the students in his adult literacy class, as they have overcome substantial hurdles just to attend. In particular, he knows the women in the room never really had the chance to receive much formal schooling when they were young and now are very committed to learning to read and write.

A proud Bihari, Abhijit was born just outside of Nalanda, a town in the northeast part of the state. His family later moved to the outskirts of Patna, the state capital. As a Tier 2 city, economic progress has been slower in Patna compared to other Indian state capitals, and it has always seemed sleepy and traditionalist. In addition, Bihar has some of the worst human condition indicators in India, which shows the scope of progress needed to address the underlying issue of poverty. For example, a baby born in Bihar is three times more likely to die before their fifth birthday than a baby born in Kerala (a state on the southwest coast of India). The percentage of people living in extreme poverty in Bihar is one of the highest out of the states in India, and rural poverty is especially pervasive.

Despite the poverty statistics, this area in Bihar has some of the richest cultural history one can imagine. Just 95 km (59 mi) southeast of the capital city lies the ruins of the ancient Buddhist monastery of Mahavihara, established in the fourth century, making it one of the most prestigious areas for pilgrimage and study. Today the ruins, which were partially excavated in the 1800s, detail a complex and intricate series of scholarly rooms, dormitories, and shrines, all constructed with dusky red terracotta bricks. In addition to the imposing structure and intricate pattern of interconnected rooms, there are pottery shards, coins, and remnants of a mural painting, indicating a rich storytelling history as part of the ancient pedagogy. The structures and teachings in Nalanda were documented by Xuanzang, a Chinese monk from the seventh century who wrote about his travels from China to Nalanda in search of the manuscripts of the Buddha. The detailed writings about his travels became known as the classic novel *Journey to the West,* which has been the inspiration for many literary pieces.

In the same general area as the ancient Buddhist monastery lies an area with great importance for Jainism, another major religion of India with ancient roots, including a pilgrimage site and sites with murals believed to be painted by Jain monks many centuries ago.

As he sets up his shop, Abhijit reflects on the rich history of the area and the jarring setting of contemporary poverty that is pervasive in the area. In his field of literacy, although there has been significant progress in the past decade, the rate of female literacy has only recently risen above 50 percent. Male literacy is higher, at 70 percent, but both numbers are below the national average. They also point to the disparity between men and women, as gender issues loom large.

• • •

Abhijit is drawn to adult literacy as a way to address some of the barriers that trap people in poverty, feeling that his own education has opened doors to job opportunities that his father and grandfather never had. He has a cousin, Sachin, who is a supervisor for a small microfinance and social program organization known as CDOT, the Centre for Orientation Development & Training, a small NGO headquartered in Patna, Bihar, the state capital. Sachin saw how successful agents were able to make an astonishingly high income if they were able to build a substantial roster of customers and accounts. He thought Abhijit would be perfect since Abhijit taught adult literacy and seemed very organized.

When Sachin told Abhijit about the opportunity to become a banking correspondent agent, he felt even more strongly that the job would allow him to help poor people in the village get better access to and security for their funds—surely a big benefit. Abhijit had read the government circulars about financial inclusion, which he always thought was a buzzword, but he realized that for women like his mother and aunt, being included as part of the formal banking system could make a significant difference in their economic security.

Active only for a few months, Abhijit is steadily accumulating regular customers; each month he outperforms the previous month. At his current rate of growth, he could reach his goal income after only eight months—and if the growth continues, he could match the salary of an entry-level bank employee in about a year's time. This motivation spurs him on, as he has wanted to study accounting and work in a bank. But he didn't have the resources for private tuition, and his grades weren't quite up to snuff, making it difficult for him to get into the competitive government programs.

Benefits Day

Abhijit's agent business is at the edge of the market, where vendors come to sell all types of vegetables and household goods; a few sell freshly cooked food. The bank that supports his activities is next door, and they have rented the previously shuttered shop to set up as a community agent point or a place where agents would go. In this case, the placement of the mobile-banking agent next to a branch was deliberate. Although the bank is committed to opening new accounts, most of the poor villagers know that the agent's business is to dissuade them from going to the main banking hall next door, reserving that for people with high balances and significant loans.

After Abhijit unlocks the rusty shutters and raises them, he walks into the modest building, which looks like a storage facility that hasn't been attended to for several years. Piles of yellowed papers are in one corner, along with metal filing cabinets. An old desk with numbers carved on the wood sits in one corner, and a single light bulb descends too low in the middle of the room. To save electricity, Abhijit lets the natural sunlight illuminate the place and does not switch on the bulb. He takes his laptop out of his cloth messenger bag and places it on the desk and then removes the power cord and a small fingerprint reader. It has taken him and his uncle over a year to save up for the laptop, a requirement for his new job. He uses it to perform financial transactions for customers, such as deposits or withdrawals, much like a small bank.

Abhijit logs on to the app for his agent business and sets up the printer and fingerprint reader (used for the biometric Aadhaar national ID system used in India). He does not turn the printer on immediately but rather waits until he needs to print something, normally about two or three times each day. He carefully looks through yesterday's printouts and decides two sheets do not contain vital information and can be reused by printing on the backs of the pages. He inserts a thumb drive, which connects him to the internet.

Unfortunately, the app is failing to start up properly, so he starts the reboot process by carefully unplugging the fingerprint reader, printer, and cable for the internet; rebooting the laptop; then slowly reconnecting everything. He curses the upgrade that the tech provider announced last week. Ever since they installed version three, the biometric reader has to be booted two or three times until it works. Today, he finds that the operating system has an update pending, so it takes over seven minutes until things seem to be connecting properly.

• • •

Today is benefits day, so Abhijit expects to be very busy. Under a relatively new scheme, every month the state government transfers an individual's rural payment or old age pensions into the formal no-fee bank accounts it was encouraging everyone to open. Prior to the initiation of this scheme, benefits were distributed in sacks of cash to the village chieftain, who was then responsible for proper apportionment.

Abhijit is enthusiastic about the new scheme, as he knows people like his mother and his aunt will be more likely to receive their full entitlement. Plus, unlike the previous method, where the funds were given to the male head of household, the deposits are made in each woman's name. For his mother, this is making a huge difference, as his father is quite controlling of the household funds and rarely gives her any access to the family money or asks for input on how it is spent.

For his aunt, the formal account is even more important. Two years ago, her husband, who often went away for weeks at a time in search of itinerant labor jobs, simply stopped contact. It was believed that he was working in Uttar Pradesh—the state to the west of Bihar—but he was not sending money to his wife. Abhijit's father took pity on his brother's wife and made sure that his family sent food to her from time to time. Some of the older women in the village also helped their friend. But now, with the new agent business, Abhijit opened a bank account for his aunt and made sure her government benefits were paid into that account. He also notified his adult cousins (his aunt's children) of the account. One of them is doing well as a worker in Maharashtra (a state on India's western coast) and periodically sends money to his mother. Indian divorce rates are still some of the lowest in the world, but disrupted families are quite common. For many women without an education who are married to men from villages at a distance from their previous support network of family and friends, being estranged from a husband is very problematic. Abhijit's aunt is among the luckier women whose extended family helped her under these circumstances.

Abhijit checks the amount of cash he has. If a lot of people turn up today, as they did last month on benefits day, he will run out of cash to distribute. Fortunately, the bank is just around the corner, and he can pop in and replenish cash, although last time there was a long line at the bank. It would be easier for him if his customers spaced out their visits during the month, but he knows demand will be high on the day benefits are paid. His phone pings. It's a text message from his cousin informing him that someone from the head office wants to visit an agent. Evidently, they have a foreign visitor.

Harnessing Agent Activities

After four years of working with Opportunity International as their head of digital, I have been given the okay to double the team from a solo to a two-person effort. I assign my colleague to focus on Africa so that I can immerse myself in India.

I arrived at the Delhi airport late last night, then got another plane very early this morning to Patna. When I checked in for my flight, the woman at the counter started speaking to me in brief bursts of Hindi. It was only when I pulled out my passport that she identified me as a foreigner and switched to English.

I find that I am mistaken for Indian quite a lot on this trip. Many confuse my features with those of people from Northeast India, such as the Meitei people of Manipur, where people with a lot of my East Asian features reside. It strikes me as odd that when traveling, I am mistaken for a native, but in my home country of America, I am often identified as foreign.

I meet up with Akhil, my host, just outside CDOT's head office. CDOT began by giving small-scale loans to poor women. About two years ago it introduced an agent business with mixed results. I was sent by my OI colleagues to see if there was a way to harness CDOT's agent activities and grow them substantially. The success of M-Pesa, the Kenyan mobile-phone-based system of sending money to another person, had attracted tens of millions of active users and spawned many subsequent launches across Africa. Vodacom, the parent company that launched the service in Kenya, attempted to launch the service in India, entitling the funds as M-PAiSA, using the Indian word for money. Although the service attracted some initial attention, M-PAiSA never experienced the hockey-stick-like growth curves of its African counterpart, and while other initiatives attempted to launch agents, they were still seen as a novelty rather than a potential large-scale service.

The first part of our trip driving out of Patna is delayed by a traffic jam consisting of two trucks, one holding construction materials and the other packed with people, likely day laborers headed out for their daily work. The two trucks are poised in a standoff, with neither driver willing to yield. Once we reach the open highway, the traffic lessens considerably. I can see the irregular landscape that looks pockmarked by mud. The tarmac, which was of good quality just outside the city, becomes irregular, and our driver has to swerve to avoid potholes.

"This is one of the areas that was devastated by flooding during the rainy season," says Akhil, my host. "The flooding also causes land prices to be low relative to most of India." I look out the window with the floods in mind. The annual monsoon rains affect Bihar each season, but in recent times, the devastation and disruption seems to have grown. The year prior, eight million people in the state, representing around 1,300 villages, were displaced. In addition, the death toll included several dozen people.

Many of the low-lying areas still look damp with what appears to be overgrown weeds growing out of pockets of standing water. But as we move farther away from the city, we start to see agricultural areas and cultivated crops in orderly rows. As we arrive at the market, I can see multiple vegetable vendors with their wares stacked high. Bihar is one of the most prolific producers of vegetable crops in India. The proliferation of white and green colors strikes me as muted compared to the vibrant-hued markets I've seen in other locations. There are white heads of cauliflower, smaller than I'm used to seeing, stacked irregularly three to four flowery heads high. I spot long beans that look like coarse green beans, and there are vegetables that I remember from my time in Asia, including various squashes and gourds, their lumpy outer skin in dark forest green. Garlic also joins the white shades, and some citrus that looks like limes joins the yellowish greens. Finally, I spot some red chilis, their bright color jumping out in a sea of green. Most of the vegetable stalls are attended by women wearing traditional-style saris in a dark red color.

We exit the car, then wind our way past the vegetables in a moderately busy market and see several vendors with large canvas bags of grains and pulses. I count at least 12 different kinds of dried beans—or *dahl,* as they are called—some large ones the size of coins, others very tiny. I recognize most and know what types of dishes they might go in, but I do not know the names. I notice that it's mostly men attending the grain and pulses area (pulses are the edible seeds of legumes). Before I can ask about the reasons there are so many men here, Akhil directs me past a seller of Hindu beads, hand-carved bracelets, and necklaces to aid in prayers. We turn left down a dusty, unpaved road. Most of the shops here are shuttered, and it looks as though it must be past closing time, although it is only midmorning. About a block off the main road, we step up into what looks like an abandoned storefront with partially lifted blue shutters. There are no signs or demarcations outside; the previous owner of this shopfront took his sign away long ago.

Akhil tries to introduce me to Abhijit, who is in the midst of a transaction with an older man.

"Don't interrupt him," I quickly interject. "I want to watch the transaction unfold."

Akhil turns to me with a puzzled look and hesitates, but gestures for us to step to the side. He flicks a switch that lights a naked bulb. I scan the area quickly and notice that this seems less like a financial services point and more like a place you might visit a clerk or a notary. An older man is perched on the lone chair. I see no visible signs or notifications that would tell people they are in an agent's office. On the desk are a green receipt book and pen; Abhijit's laptop computer, which has a dongle or thumb drive plugged in; and his biometric reader that he is frantically unplugging and plugging into its USB port.

"Do you provide posters, so customers know this is the agent place?" I ask Akhil.

"No need," he says. "Everyone here knows Abhijit."

"What about flyers to indicate the fees? In Africa, this would be a requirement to show the fees transparently."

Akhil seems surprised. "Oh, I hadn't thought of that."

There seems to be some confusion and frustration, and Abhijit tells the man to wait while he reboots his computer. I hear a loud sigh and what is likely swearing. I ask Akhil what type of transaction the older man is trying to do, and he speaks some Hindi to Abhijit.

"The old man is trying to open a bank account." Akhil hesitates. "The thumbprint authentication is giving some problems, so Abhijit is rebooting everything and will try again," Akhil says. "They are trying to open an Aadhaar-enabled account. Don't worry, the biometric problem has only occurred since the most recent upgrade last week. I'm sure it will be fine. Rebooting usually resolves it."

While the early days of Aadhaar were relatively muted, the numbers of people using it increased rapidly after several state governments ran campaigns to have comprehensive registration. As more people were on the system, services like healthcare and transportation became increasingly tied to the ID service for all Indian citizens. At the time in 2016 when I was in Patna, Aadhaar had surpassed one billion people, making it the largest ID system in the world.

After rebooting twice, the biometric reader and core software seems to be behaving well enough. It takes about 15 minutes for Abhijit to finish registering the older man for his account. Before I can ask any questions, an older woman accompanied by her son walks in. I move to stand behind Abhijit so I can glance at his screen to get a better idea of how his agent software works. The son speaks a few garbled phrases, and Abhijit extends the biometric reader, a small box no bigger than a two-inch cube, toward the older woman. She places her finger on the cube, and after waiting for about 10 to 15 seconds, I see that Abhijit's screen is populating with some information. They continue to speak in hushed tones, and Abhijit opens his drawer, withdraws a tin box, and carefully counts out 200 rupees and hands them to the woman. She hands over a savings passbook, and he writes the information down for her regarding the transaction and signs the passbook.

I notice numerous operational steps that could be improved but want to probe the passbook. "Could he use electronic receipts?"

"We've tried different things," says Akhil, "but the women insisted on keeping the passbooks."

I am puzzled. Women of that age in this area likely do not have formal education. "Can she read the contents?"

"No, but she has been told by her family to look for an entry in the passbook," Akhil replies.

I ask Abhijit to tell me about his typical day and how many transactions he normally conducts. A bit shy, he hands me his logbook, which is a green ledger filled with careful lettering. I look at the previous day's transactions, which were of small-scale deposits and withdrawals, mostly in the 100- to 200-rupee range. They show that people were usually accessing funds deposited through the government benefit scheme or funds sent from a relative working as migrant labor in another state.

"Do you know most of the people who come in?" I ask.

Abhijit speaks softly. "Yes, in the village we all know each other. Many of the women will not have a son like this woman did, so I will help them with the steps."

"You help them with the steps?" I echo as he nods.

His response reminds me of Ruchi, the older woman in Bhopal who made an eerily similar remark: "*Someone has to help me*," she said, referring to needing assistance to make a simple phone call.

I pause and scribble some notes. If agents in this area could be cultivated to provide the necessary link of assistance, the challenges and barriers faced by the women who had never been to school could be overcome. For the first time since I saw the extent of the cultural and gender issues in Bhopal, I feel some signs of encouragement.

"How many agents have you recruited to date?" I ask Akhil.

"Around a thousand, but this is just in two states," he says. "There is considerable demand from many banks to set up agents. We could easily double the number in a year."

I smile. I picture Ruchi's face, etched with wrinkles of life experience, and realize the system Abhijit and his fellow agents are part of is imperfect, but with a few changes, it could be highly scalable.

"What percentage of your agents are women?" I continue.

"Very few," replies Akhil slowly. "But now that you mention it, we could increase the usage of the service by women if there were more female agents." He continues to ponder this and smiles. "I think we could triple the number of agents in a year," he says, correcting himself.

"This payment system works without the need for the women to have a phone?"

Abhijit nods. "Yes, it is something even my aunt can use, with the right help."

"Yes, a mobile program without phones!" I nearly shout, startling Akhil and Abhijit.

We continue chatting over cups of tea, and Abhijit tells us more about his life as a teacher and about the history of the village.

Exhauluration

Exhauluration. It is a new word that I coined at 4:00 a.m. as my smartphone played its loud ringtone and vibrated on the night table. It represents a combination of exhaustion and exhilaration, plus a mixture of too much caffeine and too little sleep. It is the state I often find my brain in during multiday field visits. Exhauluration is settling in again as I reflect on what I saw the previous day. Condensing a field visit into one day is sensory overload.

Later that evening, I head back to the airport in Patna. As I blearily make my way to the airport bus gate and purchase a cup of steaming cardamom tea, I notice that instead of stairs there is a manually operated ramp connecting the airport bus to the plane.

The sight makes me smile. Appropriate technology wins again! The ramp is a simply constructed set of gentle inclined planes extending through a manual hand crank that doesn't require electric power or a system of hydraulics, which I know from personal experience are prone to failure. Instead of painfully hoisting my bag up the stairs and worrying about re-injuring my previously herniated disc, I simply pull my bag along on its small wheels, another great invention. The ease of pulling the bag up that ramp brings another smile to my face as I remember what a former colleague, one of the best social entrepreneurs I know, said to me once: "For several millennia humanity has had wheels, and since the beginning of recorded history we have used bags. But it wasn't until the 1950s that a luggage company thought to put the bag on the wheels." The quote, and the simplicity of a ramp easing the way onto a jet plane, emphasized the importance of looking for innovations around you and not dismissing relatively straightforward things as too simple.

My day is ending as it started, on an Airbus 320 jet plane where I spend the time scanning my smartphone for messages and emails before taking an Uber back to the hotel in Aero City, Delhi. I can't help but think about the contrast of working to set up "mobile banking without mobile phones" for the women in rural Bihar while I, on the other hand, have so many different uses for my smartphone and Wi-Fi: setting alarms, checking flights, connecting with family and friends, monitoring world events.

I was skeptical about an efficient system tied to the Aadhaar accounts, but I can see in areas where convenient payment systems were never established that mobile technologies coupled with biometrics and agents to assist those who needed help could be a powerful combination. I can't wait to fill in the rest of my colleagues, especially from the investment side. A high-growth, socially minded investment could be very attractive and might be a strong counterpoint to their cautious instructions to go slowly. I start to yawn, but fortunately, tomorrow my regional flight to the northeast of India doesn't leave until midday, allowing for a few more hours of sleep.

• • •

Two days later, I'm sitting on the bus from Heathrow to Oxford. The heat on the bus is switched off, and the cold autumn air of the UK chills my fingers. I've always found arrival back in the UK from tropical places bracing; sometimes I've had to endure a 40- to 50-degree temperature difference.

I log on to the streaming Wi-Fi. It was a long, if uneventful, trip from Delhi—a relatively straightforward direct flight back to the UK, but an annoying hour-long wait at border control. I find some irony in the fact that my fingerprints, necessary for the border control officer to check, often give the Heathrow airport readers a hard time, unlike the often instantaneous identification that my clients in India get from Aadhaar.

I remember that I promised to text Praseeda to let her know I am back in the UK. I pull up WhatsApp and encounter a whole stream of urgent messages, news links, and alerts from Vijay and many of the people I met in India. I'm aghast when I read that the Indian government has just announced a surprise demonetization, or the canceling of the two most popular rupee notes. I know the consequences of that move will be devastating and immediately think of sitting alongside the women in Bhopal in an intimate circle on the dirt floor and our lively discussion about savings. My mind floods with images of where the women hid their currency: tucked into canisters amid old crumbling boxes, secretly buried in the garden, or folded into worn bedclothes and blankets. All of these bills, carefully saved, are now suddenly canceled, their value taken away. Just gone. Life savings wiped out instantly.

I now understand that moving to mobile banking is not a matter of choice. Our local partner and I have to get the agent system that leverages the biometric IDs working well. There is an urgency about it. These people, especially the women, need the service. There's no alternative.

Accra, Ghana, February 2017

Chapter 8

We're Here to Meet Adjoah: The Voice of Technology

Afia, a 32-year-old clothing entrepreneur, loves weekend market days, as these are the days that she makes the most sales. She is hauling two crates to the market when the black basic phone in her pocket rings. She answers as usual. It is Adjoah, that friendly woman from Opportunity International Savings & Loans (the Bank in Ghana), reminding her to put some of her money from her earnings into savings today. Afia has appreciated these savings reminders, as they help her to prioritize and put away funds for a new sewing machine (that will bring her total up to three machines) so she can employ yet another person in her rapidly growing enterprise. She smiles as she remembers Opportunity Bank is hosting a discussion in the late afternoon. She hopes she can meet Adjoah and give her the news about her sewing machine.

When Afia arrives at her stall, she begins working to display her creations so her stall becomes a calling card, showing off her ornate handiwork and compelling sense of color matching. The talented dressmaker has become very popular lately after having crafted garments for several widely attended big events. She spent all the previous week making three garments for an upcoming wedding. She loves creating geometric patterned fabrics infused with the colors of the Ghanaian flag, and using accented basic white for a bridal party.

She gathers all of the garments she was working on, the lively dresses and headwraps, and neatly folds them into three piles sorted by size. Afia continues to fold and stack garments, choosing the most colorful for display. She sets up sample garments and fabrics to show off the beautiful patterns and contrasting colors; her favorites are gold and a turquoise-like blue. Her specialty is in taking a customer's favorite fabrics and patterns, even if they are from other parts of Africa, and making a garment that has a local cut and fit. This combination gives clothing made by Afia a cosmopolitan feel while still adhering to local traditions.

She has suppliers that bring fabrics from Nigeria, Togo, and even farther afield. A few years ago, the government and many businesses encouraged casual-dress Fridays for office workers, which was a boon to her business. Afia would obtain fabrics that replicated the logo of well-known companies and fashion them into bespoke dresses, jackets, and head dressings. She wants to expand on this commercial side of the business, perhaps obtaining a multinational corporation as a customer one day, as that would give her steady year-round business, less dependent on festival seasons and weddings.

In every direction around her in the market, people seem to be immersed in their mobile phones, using them for everything from mobile-assisted health to financial services and social networking. Billboards are plastered with ads from the various telecom services, and when she looks just beyond the main market area, Afia can see not one but four mobile masts right next to each other. The masts—or poles, in this case—are the attachment point for antennae where mobile signals are received and transmitted. While in theory these masts could be shared by multiple providers, that practice was not common in the early days of mobile expansion in Ghana or around the world. Hence there are clusters of masts found in lots of places.

Mobile phone expansion in West Africa lagged behind East Africa initially, but growth has been consistent over the past few years. West African trends in mobile usage have tracked the demographic trajectories and point to some of the differences between the region (including all of sub-Saharan Africa) and places such as the US and Europe. While rich countries experienced significant uptake of the smartphone, the over-50s cohort has been responsible for much of this growth in developed markets, reflecting graying populations and a discomfort level among older people with older, more basic technology. In most countries in West Africa, roughly half of the population is under the age of 18. Mobile phone demand—expected to increasingly be smartphones in urban areas—is dominated by the youth segment, in the approximate age range of 16 to 35. In addition to having more years of education than the older population, the younger segment is more open to digital use and is expected to drive demand for data services, which requires smartphone technology. But for women like Afia, a basic phone suits her needs and budget.

Afia's best friend, Mawusi, drops by, bearing piping-hot maize fritters. Mawusi owns a jewelry stall around the corner, and she and Afia speak most days. They have children in the same school and share similar tastes in favorite foods. In addition to the gossip of the day, Mawusi and Afia will often trade recipes, political views, and tips on how to improve each other's business. Like Afia, Mawusi received a microfinance loan to start her jewelry business three years ago. However, her loan is serviced by a different institution, and the two women often compare their experiences.

"Did Adjoah call you again today?" asks Mawusi.

"Of course." Afia smiles. "She calls every week like clockwork."

"You know it's all coming from your bank?" Mawusi chimes in.

"Okay, but it shows how much my bank cares about me," asserts Afia. "Did Adjoah call *you*?"

"You know Adjoah doesn't work for my bank," Mawusi laughs. "Why would I expect her to call me?"

"Maybe your bank doesn't care about you as much as mine does about me," says Afia, as both women laugh. "Anyway, the bank is having a discussion about Adjoah and her messages later today. Perhaps I will get to meet her."

• • •

As my group walks to the marketplace to meet Afia, the colors in the market seem supersaturated. Umbrellas are set up irregularly in bright primary reds, blues, and greens that stretch out as far as I can see. The vegetable vendors are everywhere: tomatoes stacked into surprisingly tall pyramids, boxes of fiery red chilis, purple-hued eggplants almost the length of your arm, and stacks of small okra pods, all freshly picked. This market also has a lot of non-food vendors. The paint vendors seem almost muted with their relatively pastel colors and cans of brown and white paint, although their business seems brisk. Housewares are doing a brisk business as well, with small shops crammed full of boxes and wires and all types of small appliances.

Pungent smells emanate from dried fish and freshly cut meat, and women walk around with trays of freshly cooked foods for sale. It reminds me of the old-style popcorn vendors at the movies, which have long been phased out but always made snacks seem tastier. Loud music blares from boom boxes set only three or four feet apart, competing for airtime. For me, more accustomed to the quiet markets in the UK, it's a full assault on the senses.

I feel someone jostling me from behind on my left side, and I turn to say sorry in case I was rudely standing too close. Then I'm jostled from the right side, and I realize that here in Accra, in this market, there is no such thing as personal space. Tens of thousands of people are in the market today, some coming from as far away as the Volta northern region (as much as 200 km or 130 mi away), all wanting to engage in a thriving business. As you walk from one part of the market to another, you can't be too concerned about bumping or nudging someone.

I asked my hosts if they could bring me to the market area a bit early, as I wanted to get a chance to walk around and perhaps make a purchase or two. But now I realize why Nana, our translator, laughed at the thought of walking around. There would be no leisurely stroll. Instead, I would be pressing against dozens and dozens of other marketgoers in the hot sun. This is nothing like shopping in a spacious, air-conditioned mall in the US, and in fact not like shopping in East Africa.

The market has a lively buzz, and vendors seem to be selling lots of products. Standing in the crowded Accra market and seeing most people actively engaged with their phones makes me realize that the mobile phone's impact on human interaction is something not well understood—which is probably why all the experts underestimated how quickly it could be adopted. I wonder if the strong traditions of an oral culture here in West Africa—something else not well understood by people in, say, the US (or other areas where many apps and mobile services are designed)—has been a factor in that underestimation of usage.

The Increasing Focus on Gender Inclusion

Despite the enormous expansion of the mobile revolution in areas where I was working, 2016 was a difficult year. I felt as if we sometimes took three steps forward, two steps back. Other days seemed like the reverse. As I feared, back in India the demonetization, or canceling of the currencies in late 2016, placed a dramatic burden on many poor communities, including those I visited just days before the government's actions.

Though not affected by the demonetization, the situation in Africa for Opportunity International had similarly mixed results at the end of 2016. To minimize exposure to financial risks, the organization decided to sell its ownership in the financial institutions (our partners on the ground) it had been working with. We would continue our microfinancing work without having ownership of any of the operations. Although I agreed with this move, which should keep the very small-scale depositors protected, the sale of our operation in Malawi brought a torrent of emotions that surprised me. Not only would my colleagues and I be forced to stop many of the programs we had been working on for many years, but I also had no idea when I would next encounter the staff and clients that I had been accustomed to seeing regularly. Selling off its ownership interests meant that 35 of 39 members of OI's team of global professionals whom I'd worked with for the past four years would be let go.

On the positive side, OI's work to reach those who are digitally excluded seems to have crystallized on a number of key points. Externally, our program is still called Digital Financial Services, a term widely used in the industry, especially in corporate circles. However, internally, I've started to call the program "Digital Inclusion," with an emphasis on the effort to reach those on the wrong side of the digital divide, a more accurate description. With a focus on the clients first, technology second, we are starting to make headway, and we are staying true to the organization's mission and purpose. A tagline of *High Touch, High Tech* helps to communicate the necessary combination of human interaction and training when the limits of technology on its own are reached.

If I had to point to one common thread that is fueling the work, it is the focus on women and recognition of the importance of intentionally working on gender issues. We did not have a gender-specific focus during the first three to four years of my work within Opportunity, but now the emphasis on gender seems to grow unabated.

Even with the progress we've made, I have a growing sense of unease. A restless dissatisfaction has been a familiar feeling for me as long as I can remember. From my early school years to my time in investment banking and through all of the years of traveling to the field and working with people in poverty, a lack of contentment with the status quo has always driven my desire to work for greater change. This would inspire me to learn a new field, challenge the way things were done, and work toward changing whole systems.

More recently, the day-to-day grind seems to leave me questioning my choices. I always prefer to work and travel in areas and places of enormous, rapid change, and each time I revisit a place, even after just a few months, I can see that the mobile revolution is progressing. But in quieter moments, sometimes when I am suffering from insomnia, I have to ask myself if my role within that progress is enough. Fortunately, most of the time, I am too busy to contemplate such existential questions.

The Birth of Adjoah

As we wind our way slowly through the market, we stop to visit several clients of Opportunity International Savings & Loan (OISL), a full-service Tier 2 bank that received its banking license in 2006. The Bank, as it is called, has recently run an IVR—Interactive Voice Response—campaign. The objective of OISL is to reach those without formal financial services, the unbanked, an estimated 45 percent of the population in Ghana. Target customers include small-scale entrepreneurs, smallholder farmers, and parents obtaining loans for school fees for their kids. In addition, with its roots in community outreach and traditional microfinance, OISL has gained a reputation for supporting the needs of customers neglected by the other banks that commonly serve only richer customers. OISL's customer base includes a higher proportion of women customers and those with literacy constraints.

In fact, about two out of three of OISL customers have some form of literacy constraint. Either they have not had the chance for significant formal education or their preferred communication is in something other than English (the main written language) or Twi (the main spoken language). As in India, women in Ghana are overrepresented with literacy challenges. These circumstances make IVR seem attractive. It is a technology that allows a user to interact through their voice and/or with the keypad on their device. In Ghana, we are attempting an IVR intervention to engage the clients of OISL through a series of voice messages in local languages. With all of the literacy challenges, we think that voice-based messages will be more effective in engaging users with the banking system.

Nana, our translator, and Anna, gender specialist for OI, explain the background and details of the structure of the IVR intervention as we walk to meet Lisa, a baker, one of OISL's most successful clients. Nana grew up just a few miles from here and seems quite at home in the market. Her mother was a market fruit vendor for many years, and Nana recalls walking to the market very early before school to help her mother set up her stall and coming back after school to pitch in. She always volunteers to serve as translator and guide when there are international visitors, preferring the bustling market to being cooped up in an office. Nana speaks a reasonable amount of the northern dialect but does not consider herself fluent. She would like to be able to translate on visits to the north in the future. Fortunately, her brother has married a woman from the north, and her sister in-law is teaching her phrases.

For the IVR work, Nana says, three local languages were selected: the main local language, Twi (Nana's first language), and two additional regional languages. (The bank will later add two additional languages in future interventions, moving the total to five.) The nature of IVR allows for either simple broadcast messages or an interactive format where the client is instructed to press a number, say one, to hear the second part of the message. Because many women, like Afia, only own a basic phone, they need to press a number to interact, which is why the automated responses are designed to be used by a group where the majority still have basic phones. The technology platform for IVR allows Nana and Anna and staff at OISL to monitor the calls and to see which are the most successful. They can also identify the calls that result in people having to listen to additional messages. When the IVR results are connected to the financial activity database, the team can measure the increased savings that the clients are putting away.

The team at OISL tested several different types of messages and found that there was a more positive response for messages with a woman's voice rather than a man's. The previous December, a female staff person recorded the first message and called the character Adjoah, a common Ghanaian woman's name. Thus, although it was clear the message was from their bank, Adjoah wished the clients Merry Christmas. After that, a series of automated voice messages were crafted to take the clients on a journey to understand and encourage them to save more money.

"Adjoah Is Very Friendly"

Afia and 17 other women take a break in the late morning and head to the community gathering place in the center of the market. They stream in, fruit and vegetable vendors, hairdressers, tailors like Afia, and food stall owners. The women all seem to know each other, and the community center and the air soon fill with a cacophony of sounds and boisterous laughter. Nana scheduled the meeting during the market time of the day deliberately. As Ghanaians tend to have a flexible sense of time, having a focus group meeting when the market is open makes the women acutely aware that they are away from their businesses and revenue-generating activities. Nana has found that having a specific time to arrive, a separate start time for the discussion, and a time when the formal part of the discussion will finish (all within 60 minutes) has meant more prompt attendance and attention. Refreshments are served afterward for those who wish to linger, but many of the women race back to their stalls to prepare for the afternoon onslaught of marketgoers.

The women begin to take their seats, and the three of us from Opportunity—myself, Anna, and Nana—sit in the front facing them. Rather than wait for things to quiet down, I stand up and bellow, "Good afternoon." Then I welcome the group and thank everyone for giving us their time. I explain to them that Opportunity Bank continues to innovate a lot of things around the mobile and digital space and that discussions like the one we are about to have are a critical piece in the improvement process. The women nod politely, and then the discussion begins with questions led by Anna and translated by Nana into local dialect.

"What did you think of the early messages?" Anna begins. Nana not only translates the information but is clearly adding emphasis and mannerisms more in the style of the women. The responses come back rapid fire, with seemingly four or five women talking at once:

"Adjoah is very friendly."

"I liked the encouragement to save from Adjoah."

"I am so happy Adjoah calls me every week, like my sister does," says Yaw, who runs a small appliance shop.

Anna and I immediately notice that all of the women reference Adjoah; they seem to like receiving messages from her.

"Would you prefer a woman's or a man's voice for future messages?" Anna continues.

"Definitely a woman's!" exclaim several women almost in unison.

"If it were a man's voice, my husband might get jealous," Ekua says with a sly laugh, although several women nod in agreement.

"Where's Adjoah? We wanted to meet her," says one woman dressed in bright yellow.

"Adjoah . . . ?" Anna hesitates, not sure of how to answer.

"She's back in the office," says Nana. "Unfortunately, she couldn't join us today."

"Ahh," says Ekua. "We just wanted to thank her."

Anna is about to continue with the next set of questions on how the service has impacted the women's financial behavior, when I interject, "How would you describe Adjoah?"

This launches an interesting and, for me, completely unexpected discussion on the characteristics of a person whom the women in the room consider reliable and trustworthy, and who reminds them of a close friend or sister. I am again reminded that in testing new technologies and digital interventions, it is hard to predict how they will be received. In the US or UK, many mobile phone users would be cynical about receiving voice-based messages from what is essentially a chatbot, ignoring or deleting them, and certainly not associating the character who voiced the message as a friend or trusted counterparty.

We encourage the women to tell us how the messages have affected them, especially around the encouragement to save more money. Ekua tells us how the staggered messages helped her set up a goal of purchasing another fryer for her prepared food business and then plan out how much she would need to save each week. She said the reminders were important, not because she would forget to deposit the money to save but because it allowed her to inform her family that Adjoah and the bank were encouraging her to save—which helped her fend off social pressures from family members wanting her to buy them something or lend them money using her extra earnings. The social pressures to support other adults in extended families is similar to what is faced in East Africa, but often not well understood by staff who did not come from modest beginnings.

Afia relays the story of her earlier conversation with her friend Mawusi. She describes how the messages make her feel that the bank OISL cares about her. She also laughs as she tells us of how Mawusi seems a bit jealous. "Mawusi did not receive any calls from Adjoah," Afia says.

The very congenial, competitive nature between Afia and her best friend seems to be key to the success of the IVR messages. They represent a way to differentiate service and to make OISL's customer outreach have more premium value.

Awesi, an older woman dressed in bright blue, echoes Afia's sense that the messages make her feel as if the bank cares about her. After missing two regular group meetings recently, Awesi received a call from Adjoah that noted her absences and asked her to contact the bank if there was something wrong. She went to the bank branch in the market and told the manager that she had been in a car accident, but she was now recovering well. With knowledge of the car accident, the credit officer at the bank was able to reschedule Awesi's loans, which enabled her to remain in good standing. For her, Adjoah's call initiated a series of steps that made her feel that the Bank was a compassionate institution with an understanding of her circumstances. Awesi is unaware that Adjoah's messages are all prerecorded and that an algorithm prioritized the messages she received based on her lack of attendance. The intervention is fully automated and requires no staff involvement once launched.

Too Much Success?

Halfway through Awesi's story, I stop taking the copious notes that I was scribbling, trying to capture the discussion. I am moved by her story and the obvious emotion in her voice. I recognize that we at OI need to revise and expand our thinking of the possibilities of digital outreach. For this group of women, representing the clients of OISL, there was a profound impact from the set of messages, and it is clear there is a strong identification with Adjoah as if she were a real woman, a friend. Unlike many digital services where the descriptions are often words like "efficient" or "modern," the women describe Adjoah's automated, recorded voice messages as "caring" and "compassionate."

I scribble in my mostly illegible notes "scalable," which I underline twice. Unlike previous outreach efforts that depended on staff, contractors, and materials such as printed flyers and workbooks, the work of IVR is conducted digitally with no printed materials. Messages can be prerecorded and sent to thousands of clients at once with a very low marginal cost compared to more manual interventions. One IVR intervention in India that delivered health messages reached almost two million people.

I am also reminded that for women like Afia, Ekua, and Awesi, the voice-based messages have additional elements that are attractive compared to text messages. To them, voice messages seem familiar and are infused with emotion; to the women being called, it sounds as if the caller is someone they know and might regularly interact with. In addition, since the messages are tailored to the individual, navigating a decision tree that is influenced by their actions, the voice-based messages can leverage some of the best lessons of behavioral nudges. In other words, they are structured to encourage the best outcomes for each listener.

For this project overall, the aim was to increase the women's savings. The trial has been successful, as on average, each person participating did increase their savings balance compared to a control group who did not receive the messages. And the messages also seemed to encourage listeners who had been relatively dormant to re-engage with the bank, something that could result in substantial value to the institution if it led to lower attrition rates. The surprise is the resulting positive feelings generated by the voice message, feelings that can be leveraged to encourage customer engagement and loyalty.

"I really liked the offer of training," says Awesi as we explore things more deeply.

"Offer of training? Tell me more about this," I query.

This was outside the scope of what we had agreed to for the voice-based messages. Nana explains that they wanted to do a trial using voice messages to offer a new service or product, and so they sent test messages to 300 people to see if they were interested in receiving business training.

"Great, can I get a look at the training materials back at the office?" I ask.

"The materials aren't completed," Nana says, then pauses. "We just wanted to test the voice messages for new products. We weren't expecting a huge response."

"Okay." I nod. This is another good way to think about the voice message service, so I am pleased at the initiative of the local team. "How many people have signed up for the training?"

"All 300," says Nana. "The original plan was to give more customized training to the small number of women who signed up, but now we need to rethink the offering."

I smile widely. Sometimes having too much success is a good way to learn things.

Growing Enthusiasm

Back at the head office, we deconstruct the day and match the comments made by the women to the data we had on their participation rates, demographics, and financial behavior. We are joined by Cathy, who works in the bank's Transformation Department, the area where they focus on social impact and client training. Cathy has also participated in our gender and Digital Financial Services distance-learning course, which teaches methods of adapting client-training methods to be more women friendly. She is buzzing with enthusiasm.

"I gave a train-the-trainer session last week," she exclaims. "I trained over 40 field staff. They are very enthusiastic about the new approaches."

"What is working well?" I ask.

"The emphasis on benefits of using the phones," says Cathy. "With a better understanding of why the use of mobile phones is beneficial, we find the women will help each other. Before when we emphasized only the mechanics of how to use the phones, it had much less impact."

Nana joins the discussion. "In addition, the understanding that women clients might approach things differently, with more of a view toward risk aversion—that has really resonated with both our staff and with clients. It seems to be making a big difference," she says. The data indicated an improvement in the usage by women clients, slowly but surely closing the digital gender gap.

At the outset of the creation of gender-disaggregated metrics, we measured an initial 35 percent gap of usage for women versus men, all of whom had registered for the phone-based services. That meant that for every three men choosing to use the service, there were only two women. When we sat down with women and asked why they were not using the service despite having expressed enthusiasm, we found multiple causes. The first was the lack of phone ownership (of basic phones). Although most households had a phone, they tended to view it as the husband's or man's phone. However, unlike some of the conversations in India, most of the men here in Accra seemed happy if their wives had phones.

After the clients leave, we continue our discussions with the team at OISL on how widespread gender discrimination and gender barriers are for women globally. This is a surprise to many of them. I put forward that there are fewer women on boards of Fortune 500 companies than there are male board members named John! The sound of astonishment punctuates the loud banter.

Sometimes it takes a frank conversation for things to get on the right track. A couple of months before, on a previous trip to Ghana, we were thinking of launching training programs that would encourage the sharing of a mobile phone within families.

"Do you and your husband share a phone?" my Ghanaian colleague Rachel had asked me sharply.

"No, we each have our own phone," I stated, waiting for her reply.

"Then why would you expect these people to be any different? The phone is seen as an individual device," she said. "Even my own brother wouldn't want his wife to see messages from other women on his phone."

"Okay," I responded, trying to quickly recalibrate. "What if we build in the cost of an additional phone into their next loan?"

"Yeah," Rachel looked surprised at the suggested adaptation. "That should go over well!"

• • •

We are winding up our debrief before everyone finishes for the day, and the local team seems happy with the progress of the project and the discussions of the day. I am still thinking about the way the women viewed Adjoah as a real person, imbuing her with the characteristics of a real person, a contrast to how voice messages might be received in the UK. Cathy's phone rings. I can only hear her part of the conversation:

"Hi, Ebo . . . Yes, the discussions went well . . . What?! Over a thousand Cedis?" (Cedis are the Ghanaian currency; as of this writing, a thousand of them is about USD$180.)

I hear Cathy exclaim loudly, "Stop joking!" She switches to Twi and then starts laughing loudly.

"What's happened?" I ask.

"Three farmers turned up in the northern branch in Tamale," Cathy exclaims rapidly.

"They brought a huge amount of savings collected from the farmers," she continues. "They were demanding to meet Adjoah . . ."

Thrissur, Kerala, India, February 2017

Chapter 9

Uneven Terrain: Leapfrogging at the Edges of Progress

In the early morning, just before sunrise, outside a village near Thrissur, Kerala, on the west coast of India, my local contact and translator Sarya and I are headed to the home of a local craftswoman named Bhavna. It is very early in the morning, and the sun has not yet warmed things, so it is comfortable and not humid. Without a festival, which seem to dominate the Keralan calendar, very few vehicles are on the street at this hour, and songbirds can be heard. Flowers are blooming everywhere. Outside her house, Bhavna has flowering trees and shrubs abundant with light pink petals that are tinged on the tips with a reddish purple. Before I get the chance to ask the names of the flowers, someone unlocks the door. Bhavna, who looks younger than her actual age and who is dressed in a comfortable maroon *kameez* (tunic), stares at us puzzlingly, wondering why there are only two of us.

"The film crew will be here in half an hour," I indicate.

Bhavna lets out a small giggle. In addition to owning her own business and employing a team of workers, she is an avid Mollywood fan. (Mollywood is the term for Indian Bollywood movies that are in the local Malayalam language.) She is excited and nervous to have a set of foreigners come to interview her and to film her business.

International Women's Day, a day observed globally each year to honor the achievements of women, is coming up in just over a week. As a brief interlude from work on digital channels and gender-based training, I have been asked to turn my attention to the production of a client story, to turn it into a polished, narrated video for airing on the important date. I am both excited and nervous, as capturing client stories, focusing on the positives of the work, is one of the most uplifting parts of my role. But the logistics of having a tight deadline, hosting a foreign crew on site, and focusing on one specific client without a backup plan is a high-risk strategy. It seems typical of a lot of projects, not just for my work but in the whole area of international development. We're often given very tight timelines and budgets that are deliberately set below what has been requested. But for me, one of the hardest aspects of the work is the lack of a sufficient team, especially the layer of what in my corporate life would be known as a middle-tier staff who would address difficult issues. As a result, I often find myself working on many projects without the support staff that one might expect in running a global program.

A small-scale producer of traditional-style brooms made of natural plant fibers, 39-year-old Bhavna is by global standards a rare entrepreneurial success. Our film crew wants to capture the secrets behind her expansion and the scaling of her business, provided it can be done in under four minutes. I have a second goal: I want to see the ways in which the mobile phone revolution has touched Bhavna's life, if at all, and to try to find ways more digital solutions could be brought here to Kerala.

For the most part, I've tried to plan out my travel schedule to avoid back-to-back trips. This allows me to reschedule conference calls and presentations if need be and to be fully attentive when I am meeting clients. Unfortunately, for this trip, I was in Africa just a few days before with no time to stop and reflect on the interesting things I learned about our revamped marketing materials or new local-language voice messages that seemed to be going well. I barely had time to switch out the clothes in my suitcase.

Although Bhavna, here in Kerala, and the East African women whom I was just with have never met—in fact, Bhavna has never been outside of her state—their lives share a lot of similarities. Bhavna, with her soft-spoken but direct manner and preference for maroon and green clothes, reminds me of Kwizera, a client whom I just talked to several days before outside of Kigali, Rwanda.

Kwizera is also a craftswoman, making beaded jewelry and clothing. Before both Bhavna and Kwizera started their own businesses, they struggled to meet the needs of their families. Although the situation for women in both countries is improving even though the cultures are quite different, these women live in communities where a substantial number of families live below the poverty level. After starting their own businesses, both Bhavna and Kwizera reached a degree of success, enabling them to increase their incomes substantially and to pay school fees for their children's education. In addition, by owning their own mobile phone, both women utilize a high degree of advanced technology in their everyday lives, even if they don't understand what's inside their devices or how the technologies actually work.

Like Kwizera, Bhavna has her own mobile phone (her husband has his own phone as well). However, unlike Kwizera, Bhavna decided to invest in a smartphone. I am accustomed to seeing mostly basic or feature phones on my visits to women like Bhavna, so I was not expecting her to have a smartphone. However, I have to remind myself that the same rules of thumb apply to consumers all around the world, at all income levels. Like millions of other consumers around the world, Bhavna and her family aspired to own smartphones, and when the devices became affordable, they saw enough value in investing in a handset that they saved for several months to make the purchase.

With capital costs for smartphone handsets coming down, the phones available to Bhavna seemed affordable to her since she would use it frequently. In addition, with the highly competitive market in India, the cost of data needed to support a smartphone was (and still is) among the lowest in the world. Unfortunately, very few parts of the developing world have similar low-cost data charges, making smartphone penetration levels specific to each market or country.

On our visit, Bhavna introduces us to her 16-year-old daughter, Rohini, who attends a non-government school and is top of her class. I am keen to explore Rohini's familiarity with smartphones, as she is of an age and education level to have a good degree of expertise. "Can you show me the main apps you use?" I ask her.

"My favorites are the language apps and some social media sites," says Rohini as her fingers fly over the screen. She takes me through several sites and shows me that many soap operas are streamed for free on some social media sites.

"Many of the women in the marketplace will catch up on their shows when business is slow," says Rohini. Then, remembering that we are there to film her mother's business and financial services, the teenager quickly pivots to show us the banking app and financial calculators.

"My daughter helps with the financial recordkeeping," supplies Bhavna, who had stepped away to prepare tea for us. Rohini enjoys helping her mother navigate apps on the phone with the fluency of a digital native. Like many families that I've met, the children in the family have had more years of education and are less intimidated by the technology.

While we wait for the cameraman, who is running late, I turn to Bhavna and ask her to show me how she uses her smartphone. She takes me through the things that she tends to check every day, including the weather and her banking app, which shows her bank balance and recent transactions. We also look at information about her daughter's school and the local app indicating where the next festival activities will be held. A calculator and a calendar to schedule meetings are also important to her in the management of her business.

"Do you watch soap operas through social media?" I ask.

"Of course, all of the women in the marketplace do this. Lunchtime, a group of four of us will get together to catch the latest episode. It is free. Otherwise, the data charges would be too expensive for me."

In India, the smartphone has experienced a huge growth in ownership in the last few years, and this exposes a distinct divide. On the one hand, usage of the smartphone among middle- and upper-class Indians appears very similar to that in any other country, with penetration growing rapidly from 2013 to 2017. Apps proliferated in both the well-known and local brands. For example, for ridesharing, Uber India is very popular, ratcheting up five million rides per year. But its local Indian counterpart, Ola Cabs, India, is even more popular, with nearly double the ridership. In e-commerce, Amazon India thrives in urban areas; Flipkart, the local variant, is also extremely popular. Indians have seized on the smartphone and integrated it into their everyday lives, using it for everything from watching the soap operas that Bhavna enjoys to online matchmaking.

A controversial scheme started by Facebook in 2015 encouraged the mobile network operators to allow links to video clips through the social networking site, inadvertently creating a loophole where individuals could stream their favorite soap operas and movie clips with data charges paid for by the MNO. This feature fueled massive growth of smartphone ownership and data usage in the next few years. (By 2019, an estimated 30 percent of all mobile phones in India, a number that continues to grow, will be smartphones.

However, these services and the smartphone will generally only reach a portion of India, mostly urban, mostly middle and upper class, and mostly male.) I am happy that Bhavna defied the odds and equipped herself with a smartphone, although I know that she is not representative, especially of women in other parts of India who do not yet have any device or the skills needed to operate even a basic phone. I am struck by the differences I can see in Bhavna's life compared to some of the women I have met in India.

On Set

Before I get a chance to ask more questions, the filmmaker and cameraman arrive. They set up and ask Bhavna and her workers to continue as if it's a normal day while they capture background footage. The bulky camera zooms in on the rapid hand motions of the workers tying dried fronds together and shaping the brooms. The *click, click, click* of the stamping machine, which creates plastic ties, hums rhythmically in the background.

Then the interviewer begins with a series of questions. "When did you start making brooms?"

Bhavna recites the story of how she started her own business about a decade ago with a small-scale loan from a microfinance provider known as the Evangelical Social Action Forum, or ESAF (an organization I will visit later in the day). Her microloan was the equivalent of USD$300. She started working on her own, making the handmade brooms of straw and plastic binding. Well known for her handicraft, Bhavna found that her brooms sold well at festivals and to friends and family. Within one year she had hired another woman to help her with her business. Within three years she had hired two additional women and had purchased a mechanized stapler to help her secure the handles.

She met with store proprietors who indicated if she had good quality control, they would stock her brooms and introduce her to a vast new customer base. Confident and articulate, Bhavna then chronicles how she rethought and remade her business practices to address this additional demand.

"How many different types of brooms do you make?" asks the interviewer.

"I used to make a wide range," says Bhavna, "but I've narrowed down to the three most popular styles."

"Only three?"

"It's more important to have high quality that is dependable," says Bhavna with all the wisdom of a manufacturing engineer, understanding that more styles do not result in either a better product or an improvement in sales.

She explains that it was in year 5 her role shifted from a manufacturer of brooms to that of a quality inspector. At that time she standardized the brooms, using only three different styles. She also added hygiene measures for all workers, having them wear hairnets and follow strict handwashing procedures, and she placed the finished brooms in protectors. Now in year 10, and with all of these measures in place and many stores stocking her product, Bhavna is able to hire nine women to work with her. Most people would no longer call her business "small scale" but something a bit larger.

Although Bhavna's process of making brooms would still be classified as an artisanal process and is still largely manual, I am struck by how similar some of the steps she took to grow underlie the principles of mass production. In her business this includes standardization of product, specialization of labor, and the consistent application of other efficient best practices. When I ask Bhavna to say more about why she makes only three models of her brooms, she responds that standardizing the product helps to keep costs down, and she wants her brooms to be affordable for a wide range of customers. These core production principles have allowed Bhavna to scale up her business and to cater to dozens of small shops that now carry her product.

Mass Production Brings Smartphones to a Wider Audience

These same principles of mass production are critical to making the smartphone that Bhavna carries in her right pocket attractive and, more importantly, affordable. Mass production has allowed a very large number of standardized devices to be produced each year along automated assembly lines, reducing the cost to the consumer. The highest selling handset was the Nokia 1100 (and 1110) series; over 500 million of these basic handsets were sold in the early 2000s. Nokia encouraged buyers to customize their basic handsets by selecting alternative-colored covers, phone cases, and bespoke ringtones. By contrast, the most popular smartphone has been the iPhone 6, with over 220 million units sold.

In 2007, 122 million smartphones were produced and purchased globally; five years later this grew to 680 million a year. By the time Bhavna purchased her phone in 2017, the number of smartphone sales had plateaued at 1.5 billion per annum and since then has remained relatively flat due to market saturation. This is especially true among populations across the developed world and China, where practically everyone has a smartphone handset. By producing a large number of handsets and capitalizing on mass production techniques, manufacturers have been able to keep handset costs low, and from a measurement of computing power, the costs of phones (and computers) have decreased over time. In addition, the competitive landscape of service providers in India keeps data costs contained, making the maintenance and upkeep for a smartphone feasible for more and more people each year.

The degree of standardization surprises most people when they learn that many smartphones contain internal components that are present but not turned on in certain markets due to cultural custom or regulatory compliance. In contrast to a basic phone, Bhavna's smartphone has 256 billion transistors, and the complexity ranges into 2,500 or more patents. The smartphone also allows developers—those who want a share of Bhavna's time, attention, or possibly stream of money in subscription fees—to create applications, or apps, fashioned to appeal to users. The weather app and social media apps that are in the local language are examples of apps that Bhavna uses. Her phone apps are significantly different than mine, although our core phones are standardized.

Next year, when her daughter graduates from secondary school, Bhavna and her husband plan on gifting Rohini with her own phone. They want to acknowledge her academic achievements, and they also want her to be able to be in touch as she ventures off to college or other tertiary education. Given that mass production has reduced the cost of smartphones available in India, Rohini will be receiving a smartphone just like the one her mother and her father have—although, given that it will be new, it will probably have many more features and substantially more computing power.

• • •

Seated outside Bhavna's broom-making area, we watch the raw footage that the filmmakers have collected. There are some amazing interview moments that unfolded organically, like Bhavna talking about her pride in being a woman entrepreneur and helping to provide a future in higher education for her daughter. I am excited about the footage showing training on digital tools and the use of cards along with a point-of-sale machine, such as a reader or biometric device, to process the payment. All too often I've found many foreign visitors to the places where we work are so captivated by the high degree of digitization and phone penetration they see that they forget to capture the actual work in pictures. The filmmaker tells Bhavna the outline of the story he is planning to weave and edit into the video, and she lets out a giggle.

"You could be a Mollywood artist," says Bhavna. "Keralan films are notable within the Indian filmmaking industry for their emphasis on realistic storytelling and advanced film techniques."

The Eyes Have It

With the principal filming finished, Sarya and I leave Bhavna and her workers to fulfill an urgent sales order, and we go to visit a microfinance group, similar to the group Bhavna joined about a decade ago (and is still a part of). Before we depart, Bhavna shows me the area we are traveling to using the map app on her phone. She knows it well, as it is an area where many buyers of her brooms live. We are going to see the latest mobile and digital implementations that the group ESAF, the local financial services partner, has put in place.

On the way, I check my emails on my phone. I have received a message indicating that a money transfer that I had attempted the night before failed. Away from the field work, my husband and I are in the process of purchasing an apartment in Oxford. The process of arranging funds from our US-based accounts to be moved to our accounts in the UK for the deposit seems to be caught in a vortex of antiquated banking laws and international bureaucracy. As a fraud-prevention mechanism, many financial institutions have implemented a feature known as two-factor authentication, an additional form of verification that proves you are who you say you are. Most of the two-factor authentication features assume you are a resident in the same place as your account and have a local number to receive texts.

I think of the irony of the expedited services that are available here in India, services built in recent years that aren't layered on antiquated banking practices accumulated over the decades. For me, having to deal with the systems embedded in the "developed" world means that a crucial transfer of funds will have to wait for a few days.

• • •

Our car rolls up to a grassy stretch where I can spot a wooden house up a steep hill, the site of an ESAF client-group meeting. Founded in 1992 by Paul Thomas of Thrissur, Kerala, ESAF started as a small NGO aimed at helping the poor and marginalized populations. ESAF works to reach people who do not yet have formal banking services, and it continues to dynamically upgrade its technology offerings. Inspired by the success of the Grameen Bank in Bangladesh, ESAF's primary offering is small-scale loans to women organized into trust circles at the village level, like the circle I visited in Bhopal, where each woman co-guarantees the loans of all the women in their group. With a high growth rate and very few non-performing loans, ESAF grew rapidly and expanded their offerings to include financial literacy training and a range of community services.

In 2017, in recognition for its work on inclusion, the organization was granted a license by the Reserve Bank of India to become a small finance bank, a type of bank in India that is licensed to provide basic banking services such as deposits and lending. Having official banking status has allowed ESAF to expand its range of financial services and to offer these nationally. (Within two years of becoming a small finance bank, ESAF grew to 3.3 million customers with a focus on the underserved and previously unbanked.)

When we arrive at the client meeting, we encounter a group of 16 women, including women like Bhavna and her peers, and one loan officer, Esther from ESAF. I notice the women are all smiling and animatedly chatting among themselves. They are seated in an informal fashion, waiting for their turn to make a payment on their loans.

"Why did you take out a loan?" I ask the women who are waiting.

"To buy a motorbike for my business," says one woman in red.

"To pay for school fees" is the most common reply.

These women are like the many others that I have met in microfinance trust groups across several countries—ambitious, hardworking, always repaying their loans—but the way in which they each repay is different. Although the women are using cash (not electronic funds), there is no use of paper and pen, no paper receipts. Esther uses an Android-based smartphone to collect the information. I saw the smartphone-and-paperless operations on my previous visit, and the data and money collections processes are progressing at a rapid clip. But today I am here to observe something else. To access their account, group members do not have to show a passbook, a credit card, or even a thumbprint. ESAF has made their accounts biometrically accessible via iris scan.

I recall a conversation that I had with George John ("Bobby"), ESAF's head of microfinance, just two years ago when he thought about using an iris scan to access accounts. At the time I thought this might be fascination with the latest technologies. But after talking further with Bobby, I found that many farmers and other manual workers had worn away their fingerprints, and thus fingerprint access could be problematic. In some districts, an estimated 40 percent of clients of ESAF may have fingerprint issues.

Now, armed with a simple Android phone with a specific plugin, all Esther has to do is hold her smartphone near a woman's face as she looks forward. The plugin sends the iris scan information to the national ID server and matches the iris with the records. This method seems to work efficiently, and within a short time all the women in the group are able to quickly authenticate their accounts and make their repayments.

The Rarest Amphibian

Seeing this system at work reminds me of two things that seem to hold true in all of the areas of my work. First, when technology applications are thought of from the standpoint of the user, they are often more successful. The second thing that runs through my head as I watch the iris-scanning process is to continue to remind myself that this isn't a movie set or a high-end physics laboratory. CERN (European Council for Nuclear Research), the particle physics laboratory outside of Geneva, Switzerland, home to the Large Hadron Collider, uses iris scan as a security feature to restrict access to high-energy laboratory sections. A few years after obtaining a banking license, ESAF has 1,000 times more people using iris scan biometric access for its services than CERN.

Sarya and I have traveled a long way, some of it on dirt roads, to access this semi-rural group of low-income women, and they are using state-of-the-art technologies that most research laboratories have not yet upgraded to. Most of the women in this group are not yet as successful as Bhavna. They are still running their businesses as the sole proprietor or at most have only one or two hired people to help. Most have their own phone, but except for one other smartphone, a basic or feature phone handset is most common.

The relative affordability of smartphone handsets allows ESAF to equip every loan officer and field officer like Esther with their own device to perform the iris scanning and gather information while on their daily rounds. This affordability could only come with the standardization of the handset and mass production of millions of units by the manufacturer. In addition, the standardization of software inside means that applications like the iris scanner are compatible with most handsets.

What I am witnessing in Thrissur, Kerala, is a rare example known in international development as the **leapfrog**: skipping generations of earlier-stage technology development and going directly to the more advanced. Often the term is misused to simply point out that an organization or country is progressing with their technology, but in this case, that rare amphibian, the true leapfrog, seems to be the appropriate terminology to use. Women with loans went from having a manual system entirely of pen and paper and physical passbooks to using a method that is entirely electronic and biometric, bypassing problems that made fingerprint access difficult. They have leapfrogged directly to the paperless, iris-scan-based future.

The Mother of Invention

What none of us knew at the time of this visit in 2017 was just how important the advances in technology would be. A year later—in 2018—unprecedented flooding hit Kerala, the worst in over a century. Nearly 500 people were declared dead and dozens more missing; 364 emergency relief camps were opened, and over 1.2 million people were evacuated. The government estimated that 1 in 6 people in Kerala were directly affected by the flooding.

For Bobby and his team, the floods presented an unprecedented disruption to normal activities, and they realized they needed to shake up business as usual. In speaking with the staff and clients affected with the flood, Bobby was struck by all of them saying they needed funds to rebuild right away. They trusted the ESAF staff and wanted to maintain a relationship with the institution, but the typical 60-day wait time for a loan was far too long. Bobby instructed the operations team to explore the use of digital data for their clients' credit history, a history that dated back 12 years. By using this digital data, ESAF was able to create a digital footprint for clients who needed emergency funds, calculated on an automated basis using advanced computer algorithms. Through these algorithms ESAF was able to distribute loans within 2 days instead of the previous 60 days. Roughly two months later, after significant business-process innovation, those days were reduced to no more than 10 minutes, making loan approvals instantaneous from the client's point of view.

The importance of using digital data and having a digital footprint is hard to overstate. In developed economies, credit scores are used to determine whether or not someone can get a car loan, get a mortgage, or even sign up for basic utilities. But developing countries generally lack the full infrastructure associated with credit bureaus, so most low-income people do not have a formal credit score. The work that ESAF did, by leveraging their internal data, allowed for the creation of an alternative credit score, which opened the banking world to these low-income people and helped expedite the processing of emergency loans.

ESAF is currently exploring further ways to enhance their computer algorithms using predictive methods, such as artificial intelligence, machine learning, and behavioral economics methods to nudge consumers in the right direction or otherwise incentivize good behavior. Despite their very high-tech approach and very efficient offerings, the success of ESAF with its clients has been of a consistent high quality of both service and responses to their specific needs, whether they be the needs of a manual worker or the needs brought on by a 100-year flood.

Digital Technology Is Reshaping Lives

For Bhavna and her family, having a digital footprint allows her continuous access to working capital for her business and helps her to save funds toward her daughter's education and graduation gift. Like the women whom I'd met in Africa, Bhavna and her friends from the market would laugh heartily at older phone technologies—phones the size of a heavy brick that cost a multiple of what she paid, or a smartphone with only a couple of functions and no video. Her entry-level device is astonishingly sophisticated. By taking part in and leveraging elements of the digital revolution, Bhavna has been able to grow her business to employ nine workers who are able to generate income for their families. As we prepare to leave Thrissur, I am struck by a set of warm feelings over the visit. Seeing the success of Bhavna and the advances that ESAF has made in just a few years has been uplifting. Seeing for myself how digital technologies have reshaped lives in Kerala and made financial services efficient and scalable is as gratifying as the broad smiles on the faces of the people we have met. But my sense of happiness also contains a bit of hesitation, as I know we have spent the last two days in some of the pleasanter parts of the country. We are due to travel north to other states where income inequality and attitudes toward women contrast sharply. The gains made in Kerala for the rights of women and on human indicators (such as infant mortality) have been widely documented and contrast favorably with many other states in India. Despite having one of the lowest average incomes, Kerala tends to be at the top on virtually all social indicators, including female literacy. The state, through its policies over the years, has prioritized the creation of a safety net and income redistribution.

For over 15 years, I have seen that the journey toward a digital future is uneven and unequal, sometimes making a painfully stark contrast from region to region. I know to be prepared for surprises and to dynamically revise my expectations. As I reflect back on that day—on seeing Bhavna with her broom-making colleagues using a mix of manual and semi-automated processes, viewing the iris scan biometric the village women used, being jostled on muddy, unpaved roads, and struggling with my own attempts to transfer money back in the UK—a version of the familiar science-fiction quote runs through my head: "The future is already here; it's just not evenly (or equally) distributed."

Gurgaon, Delhi, India, October 2018

Chapter 10

To Return and Revisit: Mobile Money vs. Demonetization

The air feels thick, like a layer of molasses slowly coating and enveloping my skin. There is the faint smell of charcoal and sulfur, reminding me of a campfire mixed with rotten eggs. If I inhale deeply, it feels as if tiny sand grains are trying to invade my throat and lungs, causing the inevitable cough and phlegm. When I blow my nose, the white tissue is coated in black particles. It makes me wonder about the chemicals I am inhaling.

It is the autumn of 2018, and it's been a year since I last traveled to this area to see the effects of the demonetization that happened here at the end of 2016. I'm in a car headed to a marketplace just outside of the business district in New Delhi, Gurgaon, where I want to see if conditions have improved since my last visit. Looking out the window, I see that about 20 percent of the people around me are wearing face masks, the blue-and-white surgical kind that are for healthcare workers, and many others hold a bandana or handkerchief to their nose and mouth.

It has been nearly two years since the demonetization when the 500-rupee and 1,000-rupee notes were canceled, and new 500- and 2,000-rupee notes were issued, with ATMs mostly dispensing the latter. The ostensible reason was to eradicate the economy of black money, tax evasion, and the use of cash in illegal activities, such as human trafficking. People stood in lines for days trying to exchange their canceled bills or turn their money into electronic funds during the few exchange days allowed. The opposition party alleged that at least 100 people died while standing in line trying to get their cash turned into electronic money. But the official death toll failed to capture the reports of disaffected villagers. For the poor who never had formal accounts, the lines must have been an insurmountable barrier.

I have traveled through India many times since my initial visits to Bhopal and Patna in 2016 that coincided with demonetization. In the ensuing 24 months, the country's population has surpassed 1.3 billion, rapidly catching up to Chinese levels. During the past two years, the overall economy has continued to grow and car ownership and air pollution along with it, especially in the capital of New Delhi.

By this point in 2018, the number of mobile phone owners, of any type of phone, in India has grown to 775 million users, more than twice the population of phone users in the US. Smartphone usage here has increased from 300 million to 480 million—although, given handset costs and the need to frequently recharge batteries, most of those users are relatively upper-income.

With the proliferation in smartphones, there's been growth in e-commerce services, including health, education, and travel, to name a few. Aadhaar national ID registrations continue to grow as more and more services begin to rely on the system as a form of universal identification. During the past two years, more than 200 million people were issued a national ID, almost three times the population of the United Kingdom. Despite looking at these statistics regularly and seeing the widespread usage of phones on all of my trips, I still find the magnitude of the numbers astonishing.

After a long drive due to traffic congestion, I look out the window and see that we are approaching a public marketplace that I try to go to each visit. At first glance, the marketplace looks very busy, returning to pre-2016 levels of bustle and noise.

A Deserted Marketplace

In 2017, I traveled to this same market in Gurgaon to see firsthand what the impact of demonetization had been, knowing there had been serious disruption. The government gave the public only two weeks' notice before the two most circulated bills in the country were canceled. Any old currency people still held after the deadline was worthless. Official statistics show that GDP growth in India slowed to a four-year low. Rural areas were impacted more than urban, as agriculture expansion fell by more than half (from 4.9 percent in 2017 to 2.1 percent in 2018). Despite the issuance of new currency, the main effect, observed for months, was a shortage of cash.

ATMs continually ran out of the newly issued bills, and several sectors saw a significant slowdown in activities, especially among lower-income and more rural communities. An estimated 800,000 drivers were stranded with their trucks without appropriate means to pay tolls, some amounting to only about 35 cents in US currency. In addition, the bustling marketplaces, where those on lower incomes tended to purchase their goods, slowed down, as many people lacked cash to complete purchases and many merchants hoarded their small bills. In agriculture, the lack of cash caused crop prices to drop and rural agricultural incomes to decline.

My trip to Delhi in 2017, although still busy, seemed quieter. The typical haze that set in due to exhaust from so many cars seemed manageable relative to previous trips, and rooms at my usual hotel were easily available. I had recently reconnected with Vijay Singh Aditya, an Ashoka fellow whom I had known and worked with for over a decade. We first met in Kenya during a collaboration of Ashoka fellows that I facilitated that included an on-site visit to Kabira, a massive slum in Nairobi that was also the epicenter of the mobile payment revolution. Vijay and his software development company continued to focus on tools for outreach to rural communities and marginalized people. I was happy we were working together again, as I needed a trusted set of eyes and ears to navigate these opaque foreign areas.

Vijay was one of the most vocal critics of demonetization, pointing out the disproportionate burden on the poor. The World Bank had estimated a devastating impact on destroying savings that had been held in cash. We made our way to the marketplace, where I was expecting sprawling stalls, stacked vegetables, and bustling crowds, the general buzz of a place of trading and economic activity. Instead, the whole area seemed sedate. I saw many empty stalls and old wooden crates piled up with tarps pulled over them.

The lack of crowds made the market eerily quiet. Instead of the usual dozens of conversations, some louder, most very animated, in multiple languages, I heard the lone metallic *tap, tap, tap* of an iron worker in one of the lanes at the market. In the middle of the main cross street of the market, I spotted a large reddish-brown dog with a curly tail, the ever-present pariah dog, who was prostrate on the pavement, paws extending irregularly to the left. I had seen enough of these dogs in rural streets and crossing zones to know that the dog was probably not sick or injured, but instead was napping. Because of the lack of normal activity, this dog could nap undisturbed on what was usually the busiest street within the marketplace, the few pedestrians and rare bicyclist swerving past to not disturb the dozing animal. After a few minutes, the dog stood and trotted off.

At the stalls, the impact of the monetary crackdown on the merchants was pronounced, and I realized the true effects had not been well articulated in the media.

"How has business been?" I asked the vegetable vendor Sangeet.

"Not good." She frowned. "It is too quiet."

"Do your customers lack cash to buy things?"

"Some have seen their businesses collapse." Sangeet then continued in rapid bursts. "Others only come to the market a couple of times a week. The main problem is those who want to buy only a little bit and pay with one of the big bills."

"What do you do if you don't have change?"

Sangeet shrugged. "I might send them away and ask them to come back when they have change. I can't give all of my small bills away to one customer."

"Can you give them some form of credit?"

She nodded. "Sometimes we barter. This morning I traded some vegetables for cooking oil, but my husband warned me not to give out vegetables on credit."

Unfortunately, Sangeet did not have formal schooling, so the concept of keeping strict accounting and inventory records that might have allowed her to develop a system of credit or prepayment was not feasible. With the 2,000-rupee note value being around USD$30, the inability to make change for what might be a purchase worth less than 30 cents formed a barrier to everyday business.

"All of my friends are in the same position. Everyone lacks the small bills," Sangeet said. "Many people have lost all of their savings too."

Sangeet's words made me feel a familiar guilt. For me, demonetization was a minor irritation. I had lost the value of the cash that I held to make small purchases and pay for rickshaws when I traveled, no more than USD$100. Certainly not life changing. As a nonresident of India and as someone who visited irregularly, I had not signed up for some of the new payment systems nor transferred funds directly to a local bank account. So I felt left out and a bit antiquated with my credit cards that were accepted only at large establishments and hotels. Many of the challenges were not that different to typical challenges when traveling in a foreign country.

When I first read about the demonetization, I was in disbelief that the government would carry through with the harsh deadlines. Surely the window for exchange to proper currencies would have to be extended. This initial denial gave way to a sharp grief. For me, the demonetization was personal in that I continued to think about the people most affected, particularly the women in Bhopal whom I had met. I remembered the joyous laughter and the fact that all of the women had squirreled away secret funds, most of which would have lost their value. The images of the women kept flickering in my mind like a bad movie looping repeatedly. This hit me viscerally in a way that I wouldn't typically be, shaken by things that I had seen on the ground. Like the sale of Opportunity Bank Malawi, there was a sense of loss that I found hard to compartmentalize and get past.

I wondered how long it would take for people to adjust and for the economy to resume its previous robust growth. I was also struck by the irony that the demonetization heightened the importance of moving to digital systems. Suddenly, all of the executives on the ground who wanted to take things slowly were now uttering things like "We should have started three years ago." My inbox runneth over, so to speak. This disruptive action, with all of its significant costs, was able to deliver a sense of urgency where my prior efforts of persuasion could not. I had to accept the fact that the greater the disruption, the easier it was to proceed.

Recovery After Demonetization

On this trip in 2018, Vijay takes me to the same marketplace we visited in 2017. I am not sure what to expect, but as we approach the market this morning, things seem much better. Perhaps not back to the way it was, but very near normal. Foot traffic is once again heavy, and most market stalls are taken up by merchants selling every imaginable thing. The air is filled with the scent of cow manure, frying food from the food vendors, and freshly slaughtered meat. The silence of a year ago has been replaced by the typical sounds of a marketplace: cars beeping, metal work clanging, and especially the sounds of merchants negotiating and haggling in a variety of languages.

"Is that Bengali?" I ask Vijay.

"I heard both Bengali and Tamil earlier," he replies. "You will hear lots of languages, but in this corner of the market, the southern dialects and products are dominating."

We weave our way through the marketplace, and I notice that a coconut vendor and a small electronics vendor have signs for Paytm, a new payment system based on having your device read a QR code. I ask Vijay to buy some coconut water.

Vijay looks at me with a puzzled frown. "Are you thirsty?" He knows I typically decline beverages during field visits.

"No, I want to see a live demo of Paytm, especially with a small-scale purchase like coconuts." I half expect the vendor to ask us to use cash instead.

Vijay walks up to the vendor and puts up three fingers, indicating three orders of coconut water. He swipes his smartphone, a Chinese Mi handset, to the Paytm home page app and holds the camera up to a sheet of white paper taped to the sun umbrella where the coconut vendor has his QR code in large print. After hovering for a few seconds, the phone pings and directs Vijay to enter the amount that he is paying the vendor for the three coconut waters. He keys in the amount and clicks done. The coconut vendor's phone pings almost immediately. The whole transaction is over. The total cost of the coconut drinks is just under one US dollar and payments are electronic, removing the money from Vijay's bank account and depositing it immediately into the vendor's account. There are no 10- to 14-digit account numbers exchanged nor is Vijay required to disclose any private information, his credit card number, his date of birth, a billing address, or even his name to the vendor. In fact, there were no words spoken at all.

After the ping, the vendor picks up a young coconut in one hand and a surprisingly large machete in the other. With four expert whacks, the top of the young coconut becomes a removable lid. He inserts a straw and hands the beverage, complete with its own container, to Vijay. He proceeds to pick up a second coconut. Quick Response—or QR—codes, black tiles set on a white background arranged in a small square, were invented in 1994 in Japan as an update to the traditional line-only barcodes. A QR code is machine readable or scannable and allows the scanner to access more data and information. Originally intended for the shipping industry to help in logistics, the use of QR codes has been proliferating since integrating their use on mobile smartphones, where cameras or dedicated apps are equipped to read the code. Many QR codes are found in department stores or for services like public transportation, linking a user to a website so they can read for further information or register for an activity. Increasingly, store displays, museums, and other institutions are using QR codes to deliver visitors to dedicated websites.

QR codes have also been adapted into mobile payment systems. These systems are considered highly secure, as access through the mobile phone, a PIN, or the use of a biometric provides one of the authentication features. The practice is most widespread in China, where Alipay, a unit of the e-commerce site Alibaba, introduced a QR-based payment system in 2011. As of 2018, over 80 percent of China's payments are conducted over mobile phones, practically instantaneously. This is in sharp contrast to my experience of trying to send a small amount of money to my colleague for a baby shower the night before. To attempt that transaction, I had to have her account number, contact information, and a randomly generated authentication code. Despite multiple tries, the bank rejected my request for the transfer because I had sent the request while I was in a foreign country, and they intended to protect my account from fraud.

While Vijay sips his coconut water, I ask the vendor a few questions.

"How long have you been using Paytm?"

"Not long, only a few months," he replies through Vijay, never stopping his machete. "My cousin who works for a tech startup set it up for me."

"Do you have many customers using it?"

"Only a few each day, but it is growing."

"Do you like Paytm? Have you had any problems?"

"It's interesting," says the coconut vendor, finally pausing and looking up. "At first I just agreed because my cousin seemed keen to set it up. But now, I find it much more convenient than counting out change with cash." Several people have queued up, looking to purchase from him, as the vendor resumes wielding his heavy machete.

"It also deposits money straight to my bank account, which is convenient," he continues. He looks up at me as he stops chopping to count out change from a 2,000-rupee note for a young customer. "If everyone used Paytm, I could probably double my business."

This is encouraging, as previously I wouldn't have seen any use of QR-code payments in a marketplace like this, only in select taxis and perhaps department stores. To use Paytm, both the buyer and the seller need smartphones, both need to be signed up to the system, and both need to have bank accounts for funds to flow into and out of. Although usage of QR codes has increased substantially since demonetization, I suspect that increase did little to close the digital divide for people who previously had no access to electronic funds. Access to smartphones, the electricity to power them, and the data services they need are still problematic, especially among rural women.

Scouting for Agents

We next walk down one of the market lanes to visit a shop owner who is interested in becoming an agent to see if the agent network has been successfully growing in Bihar. We want to see if this shop could be used as a place for things like microloan disbursements and repayments. As we turn to the left down a shaded lane, we walk into a small shop where the owner, Ashok, an older man with round wire-rimmed glasses, serves as a translator/notary for people. Two people, a man and a woman, exit as we enter.

I look around to take in the features of his small shop. As I look toward the back, I immediately notice boxes and boxes of old magazines, including old *Life* magazines, the photo-rich publication that I remember from my childhood where I learned about the moon landing, Watergate, and many other facets of history. I spot familiar mathematics textbooks on linear algebra and set theory, the spines cracked and pages yellow from age, and my eyes are drawn to additional piles of old books, catalogues, discarded yearbooks, and boxes of what appears to be saved, unopened mail.

Vijay speaks to the Ashok in Hindi and then gestures for me to begin asking questions.

"Go ahead and ask directly. His English is good."

I have the checklist we traditionally use to make sure someone is an appropriate choice for becoming an agent, but I want to ask open-ended questions to allow Ashok to give us more of his personal story, his motivations.

I try to soften the questions so the process seems less of an inquisition. "Do you have a computer, sir?" I begin, gesturing at the desk, which has lots of notebooks, ledgers, a traditional inkwell and quill and several pens, but no visible electronics.

"Yes, it is here," Ashok replies as he opens the left upper drawer on his desk and points to a laptop that looks unused. "My nephew set it up last week."

"What is your regular business?"

"I assist people filling out forms, sometimes for benefits, applications. I retired from teaching school four years ago."

When Ashok realizes I am interested in how he goes about his work, he explains that most people who come in cannot read and need him to fill out a form for them. He also explains to customers what to expect in terms of their benefits and prepares them for inevitable delays.

"What is the most common application you work on?" I ask.

"Right after monsoon season, there are a lot of filings for death certificates and death benefits."

"Do most women come here accompanied by someone?" I inquire.

Ashok's eyes widen. "Of course, it is our custom here," he replies a bit too loudly.

I glance at Vijay and whisper, "Culture?" Vijay nods his head once.

"How do you replenish cash, if needed?" I move on, not wanting to create an awkward moment with the retired teacher. Although Ashok and I are probably less than 10 years apart in age, I suspect it would be considered rude if I were to challenge him further.

"My nephew can go to the bank for me if needed," he replies, returning to his pleasant answering voice. "The bank is just next door."

I continue to ask questions, getting at his motives for wanting to be an agent, and it is clear that as a university-educated person and retired schoolteacher, he thought it was important to use his skills to help those less literate. I quiz him about the fee structure that agents are being paid, as the amount per transaction is relatively small.

"I have no problem with the fee rate." Ashok tries to put on his reassuring tone. "I am retired and have my pension. I do not need to make huge amounts of money." I suspect that he is trying to reassure me that he won't cheat his customers or overcharge them, but rather I am concerned that he seems a bit too laid back.

An older woman walks in accompanied by someone who could be her adult son. She appears to have documents that need translation help. I pull Vijay to the side so Ashok can attend to her.

Once the pair of customers have left, I ask Ashok why he is interested in becoming an agent.

"Have you heard of *daana*?" Ashok stares directly at me.

Vijay quickly interjects, "It is one of the Hindu principles."

"Generosity?" I ask. "I recall it from reading about Buddhism."

"The concept of daana is more than just giving or generosity," Ashok says. "It is the concept of cultivating the practice of addressing those in need. I have been fortunate to have gone to school and learned many things during my life and teaching years."

I want to hear him expand on this more. "Do you view your work as a type of alms giving?"

"It is a practice," he reiterates. "Something that I engage with daily." He pauses, then asks, "Are you Buddhist?"

"No, I grew up Christian," I fill in, thinking the short answer will be the quickest.

"Aah," says Ashok, then suddenly changes the subject. "If you have time, you should see the Buddhist relics when you are in Bihar. Pilgrims from all over the world, from Korea, from Sri Lanka, come to see the site."

Another customer walks in, and Vijay and I step to the side.

"He seems honest and capable," Vijay offers, seeming to sense my lack of enthusiasm.

"I don't doubt he is both honest and capable and genuinely wants to help," I reply carefully. "But the best agents are more entrepreneurial. They try to drive the business to expand and service more people. I understand why some institutions have favored recruiting retired teachers or civil servants, but tell me, how many of the top-performing agents are like Ashok?"

"True," says Vijay, contemplating my words. "It will be interesting to compare him to the women agents we will visit tomorrow."

I am distracted and not entirely focused on our discussion. My attention focuses again on the piles of old magazines and books Ashok has filling his shop. I notice the small room is filled with a recognizable but hard to describe scent, perhaps wood and smoke mixed with used coffee grounds; it is the scent of old books. It's the exact same smell of my parents' attic.

Just three weeks prior, I was with my brother in my parents' attic in our childhood home in Meridian, Mississippi. We were in the storage area to clear things out, as my father had suffered a sudden fatal brain hemorrhage. In the attic, a world away from the market stalls of India, I was immersed in much-used math textbooks, old encyclopedia-like tomes like the *Physician's Desk Reference*, and numerous saved magazines.

Suddenly, the shop door chimes as a customer walks in, jolting me back to the present with Ashok as he talks of helping women who visit his shop, most of whom are illiterate. Two women enter with a document that needs translation. I tell Ashok to carry on and assist them.

Back to Mississippi

The house where my brother and I spent most of our childhood, and where my parents continued to live, had become increasingly congested over the years. My parents lived in the house for over 35 years and opted to stay there after retirement. Both Mom and Dad had experienced significant deprivation in their early years, reflecting the war-affected environment in Taiwan. Although everything was very tidy, the large house had become filled with things that should have been thrown out or donated to Goodwill. But for my dad, a lifelong scholar, discarding books was unimaginable.

As my brother and I sorted through boxes and boxes of saved items, it was hard not to reminisce, but we only had a couple of days to pack up the house and prepare it for the realtors. As had been the pattern in our adult lives, I had a plane to catch, and my brother would soon be on call again in the emergency room at the small Kentucky hospital where he was a doctor. We sorted through a lot of textbooks and talked about our father encouraging us to study more math, his chosen subject. I had rebelled against learning calculus and decided instead to major in international relations. This choice would take me not to medical school, as is the hope of so many Taiwanese American parents, but to a life of living and working in faraway places. Amid the periodicals and old yearbooks, I came across a book of poetry of mine from my tween and teenage years. I remembered as a young child hearing adults talk about the desire to have an English-only household, something I would discover was practiced in many Taiwanese households in America but not among my Spanish-speaking friends.

"You will be treated better if you have no accent," my father would pontificate in his heavily accented English.

"But I love learning other languages," I would retort in my normal American accent, which bore a soft hint of a Southern drawl.

"If you want to write a book or poetry, it's hard if you don't have a strong voice," Dad had continued, reflecting his own struggles with having had his educational experience split between four separate languages. (In fact, I noticed an absence of Chinese-language books among the stacks my brother and I were sorting through.) Ironically, it was partly the love of travel that encouraged me to take on a career that was not conducive to sitting still and writing for any length of time.

There were many other contradictions in my father's life. A determined atheist, he encouraged my brother and me to attend a Christian church in the company of two strangers who knocked on our door our first day after moving to Mississippi. I was five years old at the time, my brother nine, and it would take years for me to fully appreciate the impact on my worldview that this couple, whom I would describe to people as my godparents, exerted over my life. While my professional role has almost always involved digital devices, balance sheets, and creative training methods, I chose to pursue the digital revolution in a Christian mission organization, one where the staff were motivated by Christ's call to love and serve the poor. This was a deliberate choice, as I knew the perseverance required to continue working in difficult areas needed to surpass the typical attention span of most companies or organizations.

In the piles of photos at my parents' house, I found pictures from the church of my childhood, where my brother and I would attend Southern Baptist services each Sunday. Although I'd stopped going to that church in my teenage years, I still appreciated the simplicity of the services, and I smiled as it reminded me of worship in Malawi and across Africa.

I gazed at a picture of me surrounded by a group of female cousins ranging in age from 3 to 12, taken on my first trip back to Taiwan. I must have been about eight years old at the time.

"Isn't it remarkable that all of the cousins in our generation on Dad's side of the family have at least a college degree?" I handed the photo to my brother.

His eyes widened. "There are 63 of us cousins, and only one died some years ago. Are you sure all 63 have degrees?"

"Dad is the one who convinced his non-university-educated siblings to make sure their daughters went to college, not just the sons. You recall, he was always more supportive of my career ambitions than Mom."

"And yet, he still held some stubbornly patriarchal views," said my brother in the thick Southern accent that he retained.

"His life was full of contradictions," I agreed.

We continued to pack up the house, and I mused on the irony that the similarities in personality traits I shared with my father—the love of learning, constant curiosity, a wanderlust for travel—were the same traits that kept me away from home and made the house and the surroundings of my childhood seem unfamiliar. I thought of all of the Christmases and Thanksgiving dinners and other occasions I had missed over the years. But it was also my father's curiosity gene and resilience gene that encouraged me to travel to a range of places, including to villages and rural

Nalanda, Bihar, India, October 2018

Chapter 11

To Encounter the Unexpected

The rising sun is already heating the air and baking dark surfaces like our black car. In preparation for a day visiting agents in the field, I dress in a long-sleeve cotton shirt, slightly baggy to provide better cooling; trousers; and hiking shoes, in case we have to walk over muddy terrain. Although it is past monsoon season, there were severe floods in the area this year, and low-lying areas are still expected to be wet.

In the car, my lead person in India, Vijay, and I along with our local host Akhil encounter a traffic jam at the main intersection as a fully loaded lorry blocks the intersection. Eventually, some people come into the street to direct traffic, but as a Tier 2 city, the traffic here in Nalanda is quite tame compared to Delhi or Bangalore.

Once the traffic clears, we head out of the capital city, and the view turns to open agricultural fields with very few people in sight. After over half an hour looking at fields, the road conditions deteriorate sharply, a combination of mud and potholes. I now understand why I was told not to return until much later in the season.

Akhil goes over the agenda. "First we will visit Krisha, our most successful woman agent."

"How many transactions does she do each day?" I enquire.

"Maybe 200, I think," comes the reply. "She is always in the top 10 of commission earners."

I ask to see the printouts we brought with us listing commission levels of the agents we are visiting. I'm skeptical, as 200 transactions a day is huge. The agent supervisors classify an agent as highly active if they complete 30 or more transactions a day, and at the rate stated, Krisha would have long lines of people waiting for service. Her commission rate would be extremely high, particularly deep in a rural area, making her one of the top earners in the whole village.

When we arrive at our destination, the driver parks the car to the side of the dirt road so that we won't block the few motorbikes that drive by. I am told to use caution, as there's a lot of mud to walk around to get to the other side of the road. To enter the structure, we go through a blanket serving as a door. Inside, I see what looks like a converted store or perhaps a deli. There is a long counter with a couple of green ledgers on top. Scattered in the room are four or five chairs. I notice everyone is standing, and there are 10 people in the waiting area and 4 behind the counter. Krisha is wearing a purple sari with a light red wrap. She has her hair pulled back in a simple bun and is wearing a nice necklace that looks as if it's made of wooden beads. She looks to be in her early 40s, but I know that it is nearly impossible to judge the age of women in the rural area. Because many women work in the fields and are exposed to harsh sunlight, many appear decades older than their birth age.

There are lots of people swarming around, and Vijay tells me to go behind the counter so I can watch the transactions. There are two young women standing with Krisha. These are Manisha and Saira. At five two, I feel as if I tower over them and definitely feel rather large, outweighing them by probably 20 pounds. I notice that Krisha, while slim, seems much sturdier than they do, and I make a note to check on this later.

"What are your names?" I ask.

Both girls look very shy and speak quietly. "Manisha."

"Saira."

"Tell me more about what you do."

"They are my clerks," Krisha interjects. "They assist customers."

Vijay chats to the young clerks and then summarizes what he discovers. Manisha and Saira, 20 and 21 respectively, are both students in post-secondary education. They each come in for about five to six hours most days to help Krisha with the agent business. For the past seven years, Krisha has been working as an agent in this remote place, building her business into the vibrant hub of activity that it is today. After a couple of years of being an agent, she brought on one of the young students in the village to help as a clerk. In the past three years, she's been so busy that she has needed two helpers. I note that the two clerks handle the computer transactions, receipt writing, and cash counting. Krisha spends her time chatting to customers, almost like a social event. I also observed the use of assistants in Africa. As an agent built their business and traffic grew, they would create employment and training for a clerk. In both cases, the use of clerks developed organically, without any suggestion from the lead organizations or head office. I was not updated that Krisha had recruited and trained clerks.

While I'm trying to make notes, I'm disrupted a lot. Krisha does have enough foot traffic to result in the outsized number of transactions. A man comes in and hands me a stack of papers, thinking I'm part of her agent team to provide service. I look at Krisha and the clerks. I look at the way they are dressed and the way I am dressed and realize he must come in regularly and trusts Krisha wouldn't have someone nefarious behind the counter. Then, another man walks in and walks behind the counter into the back room.

"That is my husband, Arun," says Krisha. "He has returned from doing some home deliveries."

"Home delivery?"

"Some of the people in the area find it too far to walk to this shop regularly, so he takes his motorbike to see them."

Arun walks up to the young clerks and hands them some cash and a green ledger. I notice they start inputting things into the computer.

"Did he collect deposits or repayments?" I ask Vijay.

"Let me check." Vijay approaches Arun, and they enter into an animated chat, then Vijay turns to me and recaps their conversation.

"Yes, Arun appears to have a regular route every week where he does both delivery of pensions and collections of savings." Vijay pauses as I stare at him intently. "This is based on some village practices," he says.

"There are similar arrangements in West Africa, called *susu*, based on traditional practices that allow savings for key holidays and events," I tell him. Then, I choose my next words carefully to not appear insulting to Krisha and her husband. "To turn the village practices into digital savings has taken some re-engineering of safety and trust concerns."

"But everyone trusts Krisha. That's why her business is doing so well. I think it is very entrepreneurial thinking," says Vijay.

Vijay and Akhil alert me that a woman is there to open a no-frills account, a recent initiative pushed by the central bank to lower the numbers of people using loan sharks, payday lenders, mattresses, and other informal financial systems. On this trip I have not yet observed an unplanned customer onboarding process using the national ID, so I am eager to see what unfolds in real time to assess any compliance issues, possible repetition in steps, and any challenges.

When I hear Vijay say the phrase "open a bank account," I spontaneously cringe. When I just moved to the UK, I proceeded to try to open a bank account. That process had an exhaustive set of requirements that included multiple notarized documents. Rather than completing this basic task in the advertised 7 to 10 business days, my bank took an astonishing 11 months to establish a fully functioning account. What transpired was a comical set of compounded human errors, delayed manual approvals, and lack of unified databases. Most banks around the world, governed by a high level of regulation, have an exhaustive series of steps to open an account. Unfortunately, such a bureaucratic process has always been one of the major barriers to opening an account, resulting in an unbanked population of over 200 million people in India and 2 billion worldwide.

Since the Aadhaar biometric identity system has been operating in India for a few years, I'm looking forward to observing it once again in real time.

At that moment, it seems there is a loss of connectivity to the agent's online platform. I notice that Manisha immediately tells the customer opening the account to be patient. It is a temporary outage. She quickly, but calmly, picks up the phone to call someone.

I ask Krisha how often the platform has an outage, and she is quite relaxed, saying this tends to happen no more than once or twice a month now, unlike the very early days when there were a lot of system outages. Alas, observing an account opening in real time will have to wait.

"Manisha can handle the outages. She is good with computers," says Krisha.

Vijay and I step outside, where there is a small cluster of people forming. The branch manager and assistant manager of the nearest bank branch have arrived, hearing there were visitors from the head office in Delhi, perhaps even a foreigner. Arun picked up some Indian sweets when he was out and has Saira serve them to the guests and the branch manager. I am keen to find out how the bank manager views Krisha's business.

"Are you happy with all of the people coming to the agent?"

The branch manager, who speaks good English, provides a genuine smile. "It is amazing what she has built in a few years. This is really important for the bank's outreach to the low-income people in the community."

"So, you like seeing all of the foot traffic going to her small shop?"

"Oh, yes. Our head office is keen to expand our business, to meet the government's financial inclusion targets, and we are one of the few branches that has surpassed our quotas."

I want to ask the branch manager about his view of women as agents and expect him to articulate how the women are more likely to trust and be comfortable with another woman. I want Akhil's team, three of whom have joined us, to hear it directly from the branch manager, so I wait until the young men finish their conversation.

"What do you think of women, like Krisha, as agents?"

"Women are much better as agents," says the branch manager enthusiastically. "They cheat less, and we get far fewer complaints from the customers."

After chatting with the branch manager, Krisha, Manisha, and Saira for about 15 more minutes, we depart for our next stop. I feel invigorated seeing such a successful woman agent and hearing the branch manager sing her praises.

The Face of the Future

"This next agent is named Laxmi. She is one of the newer recruits," supplies Akhil. "She just started less than two months ago but is doing good activity."

For Laxmi, a young woman born 19 years ago near Nalanda, Bihar, the time and circumstances of her life seem to be stacked against her, at least statistically. Born into one of the most patriarchal states in India, Laxmi was born to two parents who are both illiterate. The year she was born, Bihar had an infant mortality rate nearly 10 times that of most European countries and 4 times that of Kerala, an Indian state on the west coast, not that far away. She has a 20 percent chance of being less educated than a male and is similarly at risk of being undernourished. Although prohibited by law, girls born in rural villages still face an almost 50 percent risk of being placed into a child marriage. Laxmi's mother never had the chance to go to school. Her parents made a traditional arrangement for marriage inclusive of a dowry. Her mother was also sent to a faraway village where she knew no one, as is still the common custom across many areas of India.

Despite all of the challenges stacked against her, Laxmi is fortunate. She was born to two parents who cared for her and her sisters and who tried to provide nutritious meals. Without a brother, the girls did not have to sacrifice their food for a boy, as is often observed in many households. Laxmi was supported by parents and a paternal grandfather who felt that education was the way for her to make a better life, despite none of them having formal education. And she was fortunate that in her late teenage years, her school was the beneficiary of a computer scheme, so she and her classmates learned while clustered around a computer. At 16 Laxmi also benefited from a teacher who encouraged her to further her studies, especially in math, science, and computers, and who lent her extra books.

Days are quite long for Laxmi. She quickly checks the time on her phone, then gets out of the bed she shares with her two sisters.

Laxmi rises early to help her mother with the morning preparations, lighting the stove and helping her to prepare *sattu paratha,* a *dahl*-filled flatbread. Her mother is working on separating the chilis into small bundles and bagging them to be sold at the market later in the day. The family will have a small amount of flatbread in the morning, and then Laxmi and her father and grandfather will roll up cooled *parathas* to eat later in the day when they are not at home. Once she has woken up her sisters, Laxmi, dressed in a modest head covering and covered arms and legs, and her grandfather, in a traditional garment resembling a toga, set out to walk the 4 km (about 2.5 mi) toward a cluster of shops where her agent business is set up.

Laxmi's father heard about the agency business from their customers who buy vegetables in the market. They said that one of the successful agents in the town a few kilometers away could make more money than the bank clerks. Her father liked that the job was indoors, away from the agricultural fields where he had toiled his whole life. When he heard they were recruiting specifically for female agents, Laxmi's father thought this might be a good job for his oldest daughter. When he was told that the person had to be good with computers, he knew it would be a good fit.

Laxmi and her grandfather walk into the ramshackle small shopfront. Mostly abandoned, the place has been leased by the bank next door in hopes that it will become a community center for extended banking activities. For now, old furniture and farm equipment remains discarded in one section, while the front has been cleared to allow for a desk and chair near the window so they are illuminated by sunlight. Laxmi immediately sets up her computer and thumb drive and plugs in her smartphone. Her father obtained a used one for her so they could stay in touch, and she has access to power sockets at the agency job. Her grandfather stands to one side as he watches his granddaughter set up the computer and manual ledgers and receipt books. Although he does not fully understand the computer work that agents have to perform and cannot read the instructions given each day, he feels it is his duty to help his granddaughter develop a successful business. She is the main cash earner in the household now, supplementing the irregular farm and produce earnings from the family planting plot.

Laxmi checks her email and sees that several universities will be distributing bursaries in the next few days. She also sees the bank is encouraging savings and has increased the commission for savings deposits. She reads the announcement to her grandfather. The wheels in his head are spinning. He has lots of ideas about how to promote savings. As he heads out to join Laxmi's father, who is tending to crops, she reminds him that the agent supervisor will stop in late in the day.

• • •

On our way to meet Laxmi, my guides and I drive for another 40 minutes, constrained by mixed traffic of motorbikes, carts, and lorries. We pass by the area where Jains come for pilgrimage. Vijay hopes that we might make good time at our next stops, allowing us to visit the relics of a famous Buddhist monastery on the outskirts of modern Nalanda. I am intrigued at the idea of visiting the site, a UNESCO heritage site, as it is extensively captured in Chinese literature and myth. I am again reminded of the deep history that permeates this area.

As we approach the area where Laxmi is an agent, I realize it looks like an abandoned strip of shops: no lights on, no one sitting outside or working on motorbikes, and limited through traffic. Vijay and I are directed down a few steps toward a basement area and see what looks like a storage room with discarded furniture. There are several men all standing in a semicircle. Including the agent supervisor, they are part of Akhil's group. There are two other men, one wearing clothes that might be worn in the field and one in a loincloth-like garment. Akhil tells us this is Laxmi's father and grandfather. The semicircle is facing inward, with a large broken office chair in the center. The large chair seems to dwarf a small young woman dressed in a simple brown chemise over blue trousers.

One of Akhil's guys pulls up a chair for me to sit in, and it feels a bit awkward having the two women seated and all the men standing. I ask Vijay to take a seat and assist with some translation.

"Tell me about yourself," I gently prod.

Immediately, the father answers and supplies her name. "She is Laxmi."

The young woman appears scared, and I try to encourage more dialogue and gesture for the father and grandfather to join us in sitting. They decline.

I try to encourage her to speak. "What do you do when you are not an agent?"

"I study" is the perfunctory reply.

Through awkward back and forth in a very soft tone, Vijay is able to coax out some information. Laxmi is 19 years old and is in post-secondary education. She studies natural sciences and biology and hopes to be admitted to a university next year. She wants to become a research scientist.

I deliberately ask questions about the uptime and connectivity, partly to collate the response but also partly to ask questions that I know her non-literate father and grandfather cannot answer. She is able to expand on the workings of the system, which seems much more reliable than during my previous visits to Bihar.

"How much do you earn per month?"

"Last month, 7,000 rupees, but this month I think I can exceed that by 20 percent," Laxmi says quietly.

Her father and grandfather are whispering to each other back and forth, seeming to be pleased with the number. I do some calculations in my head and query Vijay. "That seems too high, especially the average commission per transaction. She is earning nearly double the nearby male agent."

He asks her to clarify, and she repeats the commission amounts for the last few months. I've never known an agent to mistake their commission income, so I ask Akhil, "Is her fee rate that high?"

He has a stack of spreadsheets in his hand and fumbles through them. "You are right. That seems high," he slowly adds. "But, in fact, after the first two months, she earned enough to exceed the minimum daily stipend." He's referring to a small sum of money the banks extend to new agents so they staff the place while they build up their business.

Laxmi's grandfather observes us querying the commission rate and says, "I tell everyone—all of my farm customers, our neighbors—to come to my granddaughter to get cash when they need it. They can trust her."

I start to understand what is going on. "What about customers who want to put away money for savings?"

"That commission rate is much lower," he replies. "We prefer the people make withdrawals."

The grandfather seems to have an impish smile as he tells us this, and I can see the entrepreneurial wheels turning in his head. He is deliberately promoting high-commission transactions and helping his granddaughter by driving foot traffic her way. As with Krisha, the agent with 200 transactions per day whose husband assisted, this agency is a family business.

"What will happen when you get married?" Vijay asks Laxmi.

The reply is sharp and forceful and fully audible for the first time. "Why would I want to do that?"

"She has a sister who is two years younger," supplies the grandfather. "The sister is also good with computers."

Later in the car, Vijay and I examine the spreadsheets and realize that Laxmi was exactly right about her commissions and is earning 70 percent more than a male agent who is not too far away. Although the two agents are executing roughly the same number of transactions, for Laxmi, the bulk of transactions are high-commission ones. She has built her business in a smarter fashion, and I wonder if the agent supervisor and Akhil and his team understand this. Like Krisha, this young agent's business represents and supports the work of the whole family. And the grandfather, a man in traditional dress, who is illiterate, is the entrepreneurial drive.

Seeing how successful Krisha and Laxmi have become makes me pause. I make a note to be more aspirational in my expectations for women agents and not to extrapolate general statistics to a specific situation. Although the cultural customs in this area have things stacked against women, it is clear that there are cases that defy the average statistics. Both Krisha and Laxmi can become examples for other women to learn from. I am quite pleased at their success.

The Power in an X

We drive farther north to a deeper rural area and stop by a third agent. This one, I am told, is the cousin of the loan supervisor and can speak a bit of English. It is Madesh, known as Max, who resembles a Bollywood star.

Max's shop looks like a rundown space where everyone has discarded their old office equipment. There are broken printers stacked high, several old metallic filing cabinets, some broken office chairs where the armrests have come off due to usage. There is a lone metallic desk cleared for Max to conduct his business. Max's laptop computer sits in the center of the desk, the focus of most people's attention. A suspended light bulb in the middle of the room indicates that the office is electrified, giving Max the luxury of running his business continuously as long as he has customers.

A woman named Priya is in the shop when we enter. She is wearing a simple maroon sari, carries a plastic bag, and has a red dot in her hair, indicating she is married. The man who is with her tells Vijay that he is not a relative but is simply there to help Priya and has accompanied her from her village.

To begin, Max picks up the fingerprint reader tethered to his laptop. It is a tiny metallic block, the size of a matchbox. He extends the object in Priya's direction.

Priya tentatively holds out her hand to Max, and he methodically grasps her left thumb, places it on the tiny reader, and presses down. His computer screen almost immediately flashes NO MATCH in large red letters.

He then slowly but deliberately takes her index finger and in total silence places it on the metallic box.

Immediately, the screen again says NO MATCH.

Vijay and Akhil start to shift nervously. As I now know, many people like Priya have worn away their fingerprints through years of manual labor, handwashing clothes, working as a housemaid, and grasping a garden hoe to weed vegetable plots to earn a few rupees.

Max then switches to her ring finger, and after what seems like an hour, but is no more than five seconds, he tries a third time. He places her ring finger on the reader. This time there is no error message, and the screen populates with data and a photo, all information that was collected when registering for a national ID card.

Max looks down at his screen, then up at Priya, and asks what her mother's name is. She whispers an answer. He nods. He then clicks his mouse twice, which transfers the information and autofills an electronic form. He opens the bottom drawer to a metal filing cabinet and removes two sheets of paper and loads these into the printer, prints the application, then extends it to be signed. The man standing next to Priya skims the document quickly and gestures toward the line with an X at the bottom. She picks up a pen and slowly scrawls an X next to it.

And with the X, it's done. Priya has crossed the threshold and is no longer one of India's 200 million unbanked. She is now part of the formal financial system.

Vijay expresses surprise at how seamless everything is. I look down at my watch and realize that I was holding my breath through much of the process. Years of field work and failed demonstrations have taught me to be cautious with expectations. This is particularly important when a transaction requires the flow of electrons back and forth in a rural area. What elapsed took about a minute and a half. Ninety seconds. I reflect on the contrast with my banking process in the UK, which took 11 months.

Vijay is bounding around, chatting with Max, practically giddy. Given his generally cautious nature, I am pleased and a bit amused at his enthusiasm.

A man comes by with a tray and offers tiny paper cups of masala chai, steam rising from the freshly made tea. This milky, sweet, and spicy drink is common at meetings in India, and the familiar scents of cinnamon and cardamom start to infuse the air. The mood seems kind of festive. I notice Vijay and members of Akhil's team are animatedly chatting away, yet Priya stays silent.

"Could I give my tea to Priya?" I ask Vijay.

"That would be nice," he says and pauses for a moment. "*You* should give it to her."

I walk over and extend the tiny cup.

She looks at me with a puzzled, resigned expression and sighs. I wonder if I did something wrong.

Priya takes the tea and walks to the far corner of the room next to the large step and doorframe. She turns to face away from everyone, squats down, and proceeds to slowly drink the contents of the cup.

I look toward Vijay for an explanation.

"Oh," he says softly as his head drops. "Women in this area aren't supposed to be seen eating or drinking."

I turn my gaze to see Priya in the corner, still facing away from everyone, looking very small.

The Long Unpaved Road

As the day winds down, Vijay and I continue our conversation.

"Did you see how patient Max was?" Vijay interjects. "When Priya's thumbprint didn't work, he just moved to the next finger, then the next. He didn't yell at her or get upset. We should update the agent training manual."

Over the course of the next year, Max will onboard and establish accounts for more than a thousand people, almost all non-literate like Priya.

"The connection to the national ID server seemed quite fast," adds Vijay. "They must have improved the reliability a lot in the past few months."

I nod, recalling a more-staged demo just the year before. While ultimately successful, that attempt had several glitches, more than we saw today.

Akhil, seated quietly next to us, finally exhales with relief, allowing some of the tension of the day to dissipate. Ever since I started supporting the project here with technical assistance and a small grant, Akhil's been anxious when we are in the field together. The network of agents like Max—a total of 3,500 working in some of the most challenging rural areas across Bihar and Uttar Pradesh—is under his supervision.

"The women agents are doing well, aren't they?" Akhil says.

Vijay and I reflect on the success of Krisha and Laxmi, whom we met earlier in the day. Both of these women surpassed expectations and were earning very attractive incomes for this area. We discuss the possibility of adding an apprentice program that would encourage and train young women to become agents, greatly expanding the number of illiterate women who could be served.

"It's all of the things you were predicting many years ago," Vijay continues rapidly. "You remember in Nairobi when you were talking about stitching together multiple activities and players . . . ?"

A cacophony of thoughts, emotions, and words clash in my head. I recognize it will take some time to fully process everything I've seen today and to appreciate just how much work over many years had to come together to make things happen. Upon hearing Vijay's words, I realize all of the many threads that I have been working on for nearly two decades—the appropriate technology lessons, the cooperation of regulators, the leveraging of existing databases, an ecosystem approach—have finally and tangibly come together.

The digital revolution has arrived at this rural outpost in Nalanda Bihar, enabling Priya, a non-literate, very low-income woman with no phone of her own, to become one of the formally banked, almost instantaneously. Even in a society that pushes her into a corner, she can now accumulate savings in her own name when she earns a bit of extra money. In this account, she will receive payments from the government like pensions or welfare benefits. Priya will also start to establish a digital footprint, a track record, allowing for credit scoring and access to other services in the future. Her experience reflects the hope I have for all the women like her around the globe.

Oxford, England, March 2021

Epilogue

Toward a (Mostly) Hopeful Future

The sunlight starts to peek over the edge of the blackout curtains as I wake up to the sound of birds chirping in the early morning dawn. The morning air is getting a bit cooler as brisk early spring weather still dominates, so I snuggle under the duvet for a bit longer, grab my phone to read the news, and try not to wake my softly snoring husband. When I turn on my side, my phone's facial recognition software recognizes my bleary morning face with eyes still swollen from a night of broken sleep, a common pattern of lifelong bouts of alternating light sleeping and insomnia. I check the overnight news stories, including Twitter feeds set to gather important stories. In my feed are the usual number of silly cat videos, some birthday announcements, and retweeted interviews. Unsurprisingly, there's widespread disagreement and political wrangling in both countries, the US and the UK, that I call home.

After finally rousing myself out of bed, as my phone battery is running low, I move to the living room, plug my phone in to recharge it, and turn on my computer so I can start to make my way through the emails that accumulated overnight. I go to the kitchen to make some tea and notice that we ran out of milk last night. Fortunately, there's a small grocery store just a 10-minute walk away. I suit up and head out.

Outside, it is a typical English wet, gray morning, and I feel as though I'm walking in a cloud as the mist fogs my glasses. I walk past unkempt drains that haven't been cleared and are starting to clog, leaving large puddles for me to avoid. On my walk, I count three squirrels and one large dark gray cat lazily sleeping on a brick pillar. As I round the corner toward the Oxford Castle, a 900-year-old complex complete with motte-and-bailey (a raised area surrounded by a protective barrier), it could be like any other morning.

When I reach the narrow bridge, I see someone tall and thin, resembling one of the professors I know at Oxford University. I call out his name, and though he doesn't turn around, I can tell he's wearing a full-face mask with goggles. My own medical mask muffles my call, which comes out more like "mmfrgr" than hello. Gone are the throngs of tourists from China and Italy and France that normally populate the castle area, punctuating the history with loud shrieking yells. Gone are the young families there to learn a bit of history. Gone are the groups of office inhabitants out to pick up a quick coffee. The cafes sit empty, their chairs stacked on the tables. It is eerily quiet, with only an occasional bicyclist or construction worker.

At the store, I pause as the security guard, also in a mask, holds up a spray bottle toward me, but I shake my head no. I've inhaled enough benzalkonium chloride (an antimicrobial compound) for the week, thank you very much, and will scrub my hands when I return home. I wait for a person in the store to exit, and then I enter, following one set of arrows. Inside the small shop, everyone politely yields so no more than one person is in an aisle at the same time. I quickly pick up milk and a couple of other essential items, then walk to the scanner. It takes about 10 seconds to scan the items and to pay with a quick tap of my contactless card, as cash isn't encouraged. Then I'm out the door, following another set of arrows. There are no greetings, no pleasantries, no words at all exchanged. For a morning that started out so normal, the last 15 minutes have seemed like a post-zombie-apocalypse movie.

The New Normal

This is the new normal of the Covid-19 pandemic. My work used to involve 10 days a month traveling in the field, flying on airplanes, and visiting rural villages across India and Africa. The balance of my time was spent going to a small office here in Oxford, a brief 15-minute bus ride away from my home, where I joined about two dozen colleagues and most often spent the day in assorted meetings. Now in early 2021, in the third lockdown in England, my daily routine consists mostly of working in the two-foot by three-foot area around my kitchen table. Three or four times a day, I am required to sit very still in front of a video camera and talk to people, all the while taking care not to make funny faces or be caught eating on screen. Today I have a webinar, a donor call, and two conference calls. The attendees are from Africa, India, North and, more recently, South America. After the calls, there will be the constant stream of emails, WhatsApp messages, and Skype DMs.

I'm grateful that I am still employed, as many are not as lucky. The vocabulary of the pandemic has become focused on furloughs, social distancing, and lockdowns. Activities that used to be in-person have now been substituted for connection by video or audio conferencing. In the past couple of months, I have joined virtual meetups, virtual tutorials, a virtual baby shower, two virtual farewell parties for colleagues seeking employment elsewhere, and, my favorite, a virtual wine tasting, where a vineyard delivered via parcel carrier a bottle of wine to attendees scattered over 35 cities, and the group tasted and discussed the beverage together.

The reliance on videoconferencing helps me to appreciate that my digital connectivity, while still not at levels of many cities around Europe or the US, permits me a reasonably reliable connection to the internet that tends to hold out for a full hour-long call with usually no more than one frozen screen or restart. Digital connectivity has allowed me to stay in touch with my team and local partners in Africa, India, Europe, and Australia, as they similarly work from home. It's also allowed me to form new social bonds, joining a writers' hour each day where nearly 200 people turn on their Zoom accounts and sit, most with cameras on, writing silently together. I am astonished at how effective and how essential having a virtual community is, especially helping with motivation and inspiration.

The Covid-19 pandemic has also underscored how important digital access is for all of us. The increased dependence on internet access during the pandemic widened, rather than narrowed, the chasm between those who are included and have access, confidence, and training and those who are still digitally excluded. In short, the digital divide now has more severe consequences for those still excluded.

With in-person visits discouraged, and many countries going into lockdown, many services were moved online. For example, in East and Southern Africa, farm information that gave training and weather and crop information was shifted to online videos and SMS broadcasts. For the farmers who are connected and digitally literate, these services enable ongoing and deepening contact and knowledge about farm practices. For the farmers not connected and not up to digital standards, their normal forms of contact were all but eliminated. They are left more isolated than before. In late 2020, tensions boiled over between the farmers and the government in India, where the latter attempted to enforce modernization and commercial competition on farm practices. The resulting farmer strikes involved an estimated 250 million people, the largest the world has seen.

What a Pandemic and a Revolution Have in Common

As expected, with in-person mechanisms and services disallowed during the pandemic, digital approaches have gained favor.

However, unlikely as it may seem, I am surprised by how many similarities between the mobile phone revolution and the Covid-19 pandemic there are.

For one, both the pandemic and the lightning-fast digital revolution have made it clear to all of us that life can change in an instant, making it difficult to remember what things were like in the before times.

Like the ground-shifting changes brought on by Covid, the mobile economy has highlighted an interesting feature for me. When I look back at all of the junctures of the mobile economy, I see that there was a consistent underestimation of the impact that the mobile phone and digital connectivity would have in reshaping our lives, especially our day-to-day activities. While many people may have forecast the existence of devices that resemble our smartphones, very few forecast the dominant role these devices play in our lives and the amount of time we spend staring at small glowing rectangles.

Similarly, with Covid, while there had been forecasts of a global pandemic, virtually no one foresaw the impacts on businesses, schools, and global economies that unfolded. The use of quarantining, a technique from the Middle Ages used to keep people separate from each other, seems to have shifted the global economy all at once. Patterns of everyday activity were changed, supply chains disrupted, travel to distant lands mostly abandoned, and work meetings and conferences (an increasing mainstay of modern life) all but eliminated, with video conferencing and online webinars abounding.

Still, there has been encouraging and ongoing innovation and adaptation on many fronts. In the mobile revolution, 16 million jobs are thought to have been created directly in the mobile space, and countless startups have created new apps, device add-ons, and companies focused on integrating mobile technologies and services. One of the most notable areas of change is in financial services, where *fin-tech* (or financial tech companies that combine financial services and digital means), a buzzword just a couple of years ago, is thought to be an existential threat to regular banks. The mobile revolution has spurred fin-tech startup companies to explore integrating with these companies.

Both the pandemic and the digital revolution have taught me to broaden expectations about the flexibility of human interaction and not to limit my thinking about the future.

In the case of the pandemic, there were, of course, a lot of people who created a scenario where there was a major novel pathogen that spread rapidly, and for which there was no known cure or available vaccine. However, none of those scenarios foresaw the extent to which the pandemic would reshape the way we live, the pervasive lockdowns, the requirement to work from home, and the closures of schools, markets, and in many cases, international borders. It was a failure of imagination to think that something so small could have impacts so big.

For the mobile revolution, the failure of imagination seems to have extended to a similar underestimation of the changing of human behavior, including shifts in everyday activities. Currently, millennials in America spend an average of around four hours per day on their smartphones. While a lot of activities have been shifted to the phone, this number is astonishing and was not foreseen in the recent past. The pervasiveness of streaming data in public places, including outdoor parks and improvements in data services infrastructure, means that people are increasingly connecting with the web with minimal disruption. To see the profound shift, one can turn to television and movie scenes of just a decade or more ago to see how people interacted before smartphones became so ubiquitous.

A Focus on Gender

As I read about the pandemic's disproportionate burdens on women, I reflect on the global situation and on how my work came to increasingly focus on gender issues.

In the 1990s, there were an estimated 100 million "missing" women in Asia. They had not run away, nor were they accidentally overlooked in a census, but rather they were never allowed to exist, due to gender-selective abortions, infanticide, or neglect.

To be born female at certain junctures in time and in certain locations often meant that laws, culture, or custom discriminated against you in terms of how much you could earn, where you could live, and even how much you were protected against violence.

Such biases were not and are not limited to developing countries. In the UK, my current place of residence, laws of primogeniture dictate that only male descendants are allowed to inherit, thus preventing female children from inheritance of titles. Equal monetary inheritance by sisters and brothers is a practice less than a century old in the UK, and it wasn't until the 1970s that a married woman could open a bank account without her husband's permission. Despite improvements on the legal and official front, around the world today if you are born female, you are less likely to be taught to read, to be fed well, or to be encouraged to have lofty aspirations for the future.

The digital world also favors males. If women owned phones at the same rate as men, there would be an additional 197 million phone owners. The number is even larger when talking about access to mobile internet or information systems, where the gap between men and women is over 300 million. Despite considerable progress in increasing mobile infrastructure and investment, the gender gap remains stubbornly persistent. Even the fundamental way in which technology reaches most of us has been designed and influenced by a narrow cohort of young men, mostly white, mostly from the Anglosphere, and mostly wealthy by global standards. Handheld devices, graphic interfaces, even captchas to prove you are human are predominately designed by and for a narrow group of male hands, eyes, and perceptual brains.

I've spent many periods of my life in male-dominated environments. In high school, I was the rare female on the math team. When working in investment banking, I spent many years on a trading desk that skewed heavily male and where a mix of risk-taking, boisterous yelling, and excess testosterone permeated the air.

Despite my own experiences, I think I was somewhat blind to gender issues until a few years ago. Although I could see that women were discriminated against, and understood that global data demonstrated that girls almost always had poorer outcomes compared to boys, for many years the extent and magnitude of these differences did not impact me deeply enough to sway my thinking about my mission and goals.

Something shifted after my initial forays into East Africa in 2012. I'm not sure if it was my perimenopausal brain that opened my eyes wider to patriarchal practices or a coincidence of personal discrimination that pointed me toward directions about my work.

By that time, I was working for Opportunity International. In this role I was confronted with how male-skewed the IT sector is. All but one of the heads of IT in each country were male. When speaking one-on-one, relationships between me and male colleagues seemed fine. But decisions that supposedly reflected the collective wisdom of the organization seemed mostly to ignore me (and my work), especially as I did not have a background in technology. During several years during which I spent a lot of time in India, I became more attuned to the differential treatment between males and females. I started to make note of the times I was stopped—at, say, an airport—so that security personnel could check my credit card credentials as fraud prevention. My male colleagues, especially those who were foreigners like me, were usually waived through, despite offering to show identification documents after standing in the line behind me.

Differential treatment also occurred in the UK. My husband and I, after years of renting, decided to purchase an apartment in our adopted home of Oxford, England. We purchased it as joint owners, a term with legal and financial meaning. As an experiment, I communicated with all of the necessary parties, lawyers, surveyors, agents, and accountants, with both of our names, placing my full name first and my husband's details after. All of the correspondence came back either reversing the order, with his name first, or deleting my name entirely. Curiously, although the joint deed was in both names, the letters of correspondence about the deed were addressed only to him. Surprised by the consistency of the practice, my husband called and asked each party if they had a policy of only addressing correspondence to men. The reply that he received was that this was done out of habit.

• • •

I think back quite often to the day that I met some remarkable agents and encountered Priya, the woman in Nalanda, Bihar, who wanted to open a bank account. It's hard to unpack why that has made an indelible impression in my mind. First, after working in this area for over a decade and a half, the extent of the gender issues in the areas of India where we were made a significant impression on me. During the first two agent visits that day, I was favorably surprised by the effectiveness of the women agents. I was particularly struck by the family support that Laxmi received from her father and grandfather and their pride in her education, a luxury they did not have.

Immediately after meeting Priya and watching her disappear so she could drink her tea, nothing dramatic happened. We returned to the car, walking past the mud and feral dogs. There were a few more stops in a very long day. That evening, returning to the hotel quite late, I couldn't face going out for dinner and ordered room service. A young man brought a tray and explained that he couldn't bring the tray inside the room of an unaccompanied woman, a safety measure.

As I was sipping my after-dinner tea and typing up my notes, I thought back to the older agent Krisha, then to the young woman

Laxmi, then to Priya. When Priya was able to open her account, instantaneously, it was like a series of Christmas lights on an unbroken chain, all lighting up. My colleague Vijay's presence helped to frame the importance like an exclamation point.

I also thought about all of the steps we took to infuse gender awareness across all of our activities: separating data by gender, recasting marketing materials so that a woman sees a version of herself successfully completing digital activities, and training and support to create a cohort of future women leaders. Importantly, our services, including client- and staff-training activities, while aimed at advancing women, included men. It was important that men were aware of the benefits of having women advance more digitally. In addition, especially at the staff-training level, a select number of men have become strong advocates for our gender-based approach. The program over the years has become less about infrastructure and devices, more about the people who were reached through technology and how their lives improved.

Continual Progress and Change

Overall, the progress of digital technology seems remarkable. From the time I first started thinking about becoming dedicated to the mobile arena in 2002, mobile users have grown from 1.1 billion to 5.2 billion. Unique mobile users have grown to two-thirds of all people on the planet. Mobile internet has grown to 4.6 billion, and there are roughly the same number of smartphone users, a percentage that is expected to grow to 80 percent of the world's population before the decade is over.

Today, almost none of us in the comparatively rich First World can go a few minutes without interacting with our own phone or being disturbed by someone else's. Walking down an urban street, we have to look out for the distracted pedestrian staring at their glowing rectangle, unaware of the traffic around. Even when we do not think we are actively engaging with the handsets, we are sending information, such as our location, to nearby towers, and lots of bytes of data are being collected. This universality of the mobile phone revolution is unique. It bridges our humanity across miles of distance, culture, and economic circumstance. And while the gap between the life of one of the village women or farmers described in this book may seem inaccessible, there are growing similarities. Like you, the village woman feels the warmth of the sun, hopes for a bright future for her children, and reaches out to her friend to tell her good news. And today, you can reach over five billion people on the planet, and they can similarly reach you, just by dialing a designated 10-digit mobile phone number.

The world of mobile payments has also progressed. Leveraging the experience of Kenya, where M-Pesa's rapid growth reshaped the economy, payment systems accessed through mobile phones are now available in most countries around the world. In China, mobile payments have reached every corner of the country. The famous November 11th Singles' Day in China, a day of shopping to counter Black Friday in the West, has reached Herculean proportions, driven by mobile payments. In 2020, Singles' Day sales reached USD$74.1 billion, an increase of 85 percent over the previous year and 2.5 times Black Friday plus Cyber Monday sales in the US. During peak hours, an estimated 538,000 orders per second were processed on Singles' Day. Most of the payments were conducted via Alipay or WeChat Pay, driven by QR-code mechanisms on smartphones.

In fact, when I look back at the progress that has happened over the past decade, I am impressed by the ongoing pace of change. In East and Southern Africa—home to Neema, our food vendor in Tanzania; Chimemwe, the smartly dressed agent in Malawi; and others—the mobile revolution remains robust. Mobile services and mobile payments have been integrated into virtually all facets of life. On the ground, there are particular efforts in two key areas, improving the agriculture sector and workforce development, both recognizing the massive demographic bubble created by the large population of young people. In West Africa—home to Afia, Nana, and Lisa, who reside in the outskirts of Accra—the region has lagged behind East and Southern Africa but is rapidly growing. Smartphones are expected to reach close to half the population, and mobile applications related to education are particularly popular.

In India, across the provinces where Rani and Ruchi of Bhopal and Bhavna of Thrissur (Kerala) live, change continues rapidly. There was a major consolidation of the main telecom players, and three to four conglomerates are expected to maintain a competitive market going forward. The regulators have played a significant role, with several new financial institutions licensed to provide services and mobile network operators applying for financial licenses. Although the type of account that Priya opened with the agent Max remains available through some providers, the long-term prospects of the service are less certain. A ruling in 2019 by India's Supreme Court aimed at protecting the privacy of individuals is interpreted by some (but not others) as prohibiting direct interface with the Aadhaar ID program.

Giving Life to the Stories

A couple of weeks after meeting Priya and watching her open a bank account despite the constraints of patriarchal surroundings, and after having time to process all of the events of that trip, I noted the importance of keeping high expectations, of the interwoven nature of family, culture, and change. I recognize that having a technology-driven solution in places with a backdrop of extreme poverty is not a contradiction. But most of all, given that I have attributed my longevity of working in the field to keeping my emotions in check and stable, I realize there is no word in the English language that adequately captures the combined feeling of exhilaration and despair.

About a month after that trip to India, through social media, I found a local writing group, the Oxford Writers' Circle, where individuals passionate about a story to tell gathered weekly to offer peer feedback. For the first nine weeks, I joined and said nothing, then slowly started to experiment with words on the page. It took about two years, a course on writing, and multiple sessions with feedback groups testing out sample material until I felt that I had a rhythm and structure to tell Priya's story, or at least to tell it well enough. There were many ups and downs through my own battles with Covid and with writer's block.

When I think back to the early days of my quest, I see the confidence, almost arrogance, that made me think I had answers. The immediate answers of thinking of how my skills and experiences could be brought to poor communities and slotted into areas with hundreds if not thousands of years of practiced village norms. I think about the irony that I, as a non-white woman, took over four decades to recognize the importance of focusing on gender and culture and the intertwined issues that must accompany technological adoption and advancement. Mostly, I reflect on the pace of change, of how dramatically things have moved in the past couple of decades, not in a straight line but in a braided, complex fashion—the perpetual sway and heave of time and progress. I think of how women like Priya and Krisha and Laxmi have helped me to understand gender issues on a more visceral level and have also helped to raise my expectations of the change that can be expected when ambitious, hardworking people put their mind to it.

One of the things that I learned that was a key element was to expect surprises, both positive and negative. In our return to Bihar and going deep into rural areas of Nalanda, I realized that the agents we met had exceeded our collective expectations—women often outperforming their male counterparts, men working as necessary champions for the women, and overall growth of the service proceeding faster than initially anticipated. Here, in one of the most patriarchal places on the planet, I had to admit that I had discounted the ability of things to move quickly. I had to admit to myself that I had allowed the circumstances and data to sway my thinking. In my return to Bihar, I had not anticipated meeting anyone like Krisha or Laxmi.

• • •

When I started planning this book, my goal was to influence the conversation on technology and anti-poverty solutions. My hope was that there might be a reader, at least one, who would realign their ambitions to see that reaching a broader swath of humanity is more important than metrics for simple growth and profit. I hoped to infuse similar understanding that the gender gap, and all of the cultural implications embedded in it, is one of the most difficult chasms to overcome in technology deployment—but it is absolutely necessary to do so. And also, I hoped that someone would recognize that the term "global" needs to extend beyond just rich countries to include Africa and South Asia.

Through the process of writing, I've found that my own aims changed as the words began to develop. As I crafted stories of the women—the assigning of names, the filling in of their daily activities, the hopes and dreams that they and their family aspire to—all of this brought closer and made more vivid the importance of their lives and accomplishments. And I started to realize that the importance is in the telling of the stories, as they are embedded with lessons and wisdom. That the most important part of changing the conversation might have nothing to do with technology or business practices or global plans, but rather recognizing the range and breadth of lived experiences.

I also have come to realize that many dogmas are wrong, even backward, and should be reconsidered. For example, I've learned that the cutting edge of the mobile revolution can extend to someone without a phone. Many people think the primary result of traveling to faraway foreign places is to learn about other places and other people, whereas the most profound effect may be learning about yourself. I have chosen my path in life and chosen to pursue many of the twists and turns of the last two decades, because I felt that I could change the life of someone like Priya. In reality, she has changed mine.

I have long had a desire that inventors and innovators think more about distributing their creations to a broader set of users, and I often encounter university students wanting to know what happens when you select a career path in international development. I hope that these stories, told from the perspective of an Asian American woman who spent her childhood in Mississippi, who found herself an accidental technologist, will help to inform future decisions in these areas. I also hope the audience will come away with a deeper sense of empathy for their fellow global citizens. Some might see this book as a call to action, and I do hope people will be motivated to support work on the ground, but that is no longer the main aim of why I write.

I write this because one day, hopefully soon, I believe that every person on the planet will have their own mobile phone. And when that day arrives, and historians document this remarkable revolution, I want the untold stories of the women in this book to be part of the written record. I want there to be an account of innovative village practices, the rich tapestry of their successes and failures, tales of their resilience and of their dogged hard work. Alongside the Nobel Prize–winning researchers and Fortune 500 CEOs, I want people to remember the stories of Rani and Ruchi, of Afia and Neema, of Priya, and of all the millions of women and men they represent. This is their history too.

Notes and Resources

Prologue

xii For a recent analysis and background on social indicators for Bihar, see "How Bihar Fares in Various Socio-economic Indicators Compared to Other States," Rahadkrishnan, Vignesh, et al., *The Hindu*, October 1, 2020.

And also see "UNICEF Highlights Poor Social Indicators in Bihar," *Economic Times*, September 30, 2015.

xiv To learn more about Ashoka and the work of Ashoka fellows, see their main website: Ashoka.org. There are also individual regional and country websites.

xix To learn more about Opportunity International, you can see their websites: opportunity.org and opportunity.org.uk. There are additional websites in other countries.

Chapter 1

p. 3 Statistics on the mobile phone throughout are primarily taken from the Global System for Mobile Communications Association (GSMA) and can be found at gsma.com.

p. 4 Background and statistics on number of basic phones produced and sold are from "20 Bestselling Mobile Phones of All Time," *The Telegraph*, special insert, August 6, 2018.

pp. 6–7 Population statistics and demographic information are from the CIA Factbook: cia.gov.

p. 6 Literacy statistics are from UNESCO Institute for Statistics: uls.unesco.org.

p. 6 Bicycle statistics are from "Tracking Bicycle Ownership Patterns," Ole, Olafulajimi, et al., *Journal of Transport and Health*, volume 2, issue 4, December 2015.

p. 6 Additional statistics on mobile phone penetration are from the International Telecommunications Union (ITU)—itu.int—and compared with ourworldindata.org.

p. 6 Mobile phone penetration data is from GSMA and ITU.

p. 6 Statistics and analysis on global sanitation and clean water are from water.org.

p. 6 Statistics on automobile ownership are from ourworldindata.org.

p. 7 These are the GSMA estimates of employment and contribution to GDP from their annual report *State* of *the Mobile Economy*; see gsma.com. Many economists that I've spoken to would think this is an underestimate.

Chapter 3

p. 21 The history of the early phone and connectivity was taken from the Science Museum, UK: sciencemuseum.org.uk. To learn more about Alexander Graham Bell, there is the book *Alexander Graham Bell,* Grosvenor, E., and Wesson, M., New World City Publishers, 2016.

p. 23 Background on the early phones is from "The First True Cellphone Was a Brick," Green, M. S., Associated Press, April 11, 2005.

p. 23 The history of the collaboration and formation of the global network GSMA is from "Happy 20th Birthday GSM," ZDNet News (zdnet.co.uk), December 7, 2007.

p. 23 For more on the history of GSM, SMS, and others, see *GSM and UMTS: The Creation of Global Mobile Communication*, edited by Hillebrand, Friedham, Wiley Press, 2001.

p. 23 For more on SMS history and background, see Hillebrand and also "The Text Message Turns 20: A Brief History of SMS," Gayomali, Chris, *The Week*, January 9, 2015.

pp. 24–25 See "How Emoji Conquered the World," Blagdon, Jeff, *The Verge*, March 4, 2013.

pp. 25–27 For more background on the basic, feature, and smartphone descriptions, see the Science Museum, UK: sciencemuseum.org.uk.

pp. 26–27 See "First Smartphone Turns 20: Fun Facts about Simon," Aamoth, Doug, *Time* magazine, August 18, 2014.

p. 27 Statistics on first Apple iphone from Apple and also BlackBerry by Research in Motion are from quarterly corporate releases.

p. 30 Original forecasts of mobile phones in UK are from "In Just 25 Years, the Mobile Phone Has Transformed the Way We Communicate," Wray, Richard, *The Guardian*, January 1, 2010.

Chapter 4

p. 36 To learn more about the SAGCOT region in Tanzania, see the World Economic Forum report *Grow Africa: Partnering to Achieve African Agricultural Transformation*. It was published in 2016 after the events of this chapter took place.

pp. 42–43 Data on prepaid and postpaid mobile services are from the ITU.

p. 50 M-Pesa statistics to 2012 are from Safaricom.com.

Chapter 5

Opportunity Bank Malawi was sold to First Merchants Bank Malawi, which now goes by the name First Capital Bank, Malawi. To learn more about them, see firstcapitalbank.co.mw.

p. 55 Data on basic facts of Malawi is from CIA Factbook.

p. 57 To read more on the relative cost of mobile services in Malawi and around the world, see "Malawi's Expensive Mobile Phone Habit," Igunza, Emmanuel, BBC News, February 20, 2015.

pp. 65–66 For history of M-Pesa and Safaricom in Kenya, see "The Story of M-Pesa," at techchange.org.

pp. 65–66 To read an analysis about M-Pesa and its impact, see "What Kenya Can Teach Its Neighbors—and the US—about Improving the Lives of the 'Unbanked,'" Piper, Kelsey, *Vox*, September 11, 2020.

Chapter 6

To learn more about Samhita, see sdevnet.org.

p. 78 Demographic information on Bhopal is from CIA Factbook. Mobile phone data is from ITU.

p. 79 Updated death tolls on the Bhopal incident are much higher than initial government reports. "The Bhopal Disaster of 1984," Varma, R., and Varma, D., *Bulletin of Science, Technology, and Society*, February 1, 2005.

p. 79 For an update on the lingering impacts of the Bhopal incident, see "The World's Worst Industrial Disaster Is Still Unfolding," Mandavilli, Apoorva, *The Atlantic*, July 10, 2018.

Chapter 7

p. 92 Statistics on development for India are primarily from worldbank.org.

To learn more about CDOT, see cdotbihar.org.

p. 93 For Bihar statistics, see the Rahadkrishnan article referenced in the prologue.

p. 95 Details about the Aadhaar identification card can be found on the Indian government official website: www.uaidi.gov.in.

p. 95 To read more about the potential advantages and challenges of a comprehensive identification scheme, see the Harvard Business School case study "Aadhaar: India's Big Experiment with Unique Identification," Goldberg, Daniel, August 20, 2018.

p. 106 See the Indian demonetization from Reserve Bank of India official announcement: "Withdrawal of Legal Tender Status for Rupee 500 and Rupee 1000 Notes: RBI Notice," November 8, 2016.

Chapter 8

To learn more about Opportunity International Savings & Loans in Ghana, see opportunityghana.com.

p. 111 Statistics and analysis on mobile phones in Ghana and West Africa are from GSMA: *The Mobile Economy West Africa, 2019*. Regional publications are usually updated every couple of years.

p. 111 Estimates of the underbanked in Ghana and West Africa are from worldbank.org.

p. 112 To learn more about interactive voice response, see "How Interactive Voice Response (IVR) Works," Roos, David, HowStuffWorks.com, February 20, 2008.

Chapter 9

p. 134 To learn more about video and social media in India, see "The Rise of Facebook Video in India," Holla, Arvinda, vidooly.com, 2016.

To learn more about ESAF, see esafbank.com.

p. 144 Details on the Kerala floods of 2018 are from "Why the Kerala Floods Prove So Deadly," BBC News, August 21, 2018.

p. 147 The original quote is "The future is already here—it's just not evenly distributed," attributed to science-fiction author William Gibson in *The Economist*, December 4, 2002.

Chapter 10

p. 150 To read an analysis of what happened in the economy and graphs about the disruptive effects of the demonetization, see "Cash and the Economy: Evidence from India's Demonetization," Chodorow-Reich, Gabriel, *VoxEU CEPR*, August 20, 2019.

p. 150 To read another analysis of the demonetization, see "Demonetisation Drive That Cost India 1.5M Jobs Fails to Uncover 'Black Money,'" Safi, Michael, *The Guardian*, August 30, 2018.

p. 156 For more information on QR codes, see "QR Codes Explained," Turner, Mark, techspot.com, September 3, 2018.

p. 158 Alibaba statistics are from "Alibaba statistics, users and counts," Smith, Craig, expandedramblings.com, updated May 31, 2021.

Epilogue

p. 195 For statistics and more on the Indian farmer strikes, see "Nationwide Farmers' Strike Shuts Down Large Parts of India," Ellis-Petersen, Hanna, *The Guardian*, December 8, 2020.

p. 197 Data on current usage on mobile phones is from "Which Generation Is Most Dependent on Smartphones? Hint: They're Young," Shibu, Sherin, *PC Magazine UK*, November 20, 2020.

p. 198 See this essay on missing women and female infanticide: "More Than 100 Million Women Are Missing," Sen, Amartya, *The New York Review*, December 20, 1990.

p. 199 Data on gender gap is from the GSMA, *The Mobile Gender Gap Report 2020*, found on gsma.com. This publication is updated periodically.

p. 199 For more detail on gender bias in the tech industry, see *Invisible Women*, Criado Perez, Caroline, Chatto & Windus Press, 2019, especially chapter 9.

p. 202 Update on mobile data and statistics is from *The Mobile Economy 2021*, issued by the GSMA: gsma.com. The publication is updated annually and issued each February.

p. 203 For data and background on Chinese Singles' Day sales, see "Staggering Singles' Day Facts Every Retailer Should Know," from Queue-It blog, December 11, 2020.

p. 204 Update on the Supreme Court ruling on the Aadhaar initial analysis can be found at "What Supreme Court's Aadhaar Verdict Means for You: 10 Points," Livemint.com, September 26, 2018.

To learn more about additional partner organizations that were part of the field work, see the following:

Sinapi Aba Savings and Loans in Ghana: sinapiaba.com

Opportunity Bank Uganda: opportunitybank.co.ug

Urwego Bank in Rwanda: urwegobank.com

Dia Vikas Capital in India: dia-vikas.org

Acknowledgments

I must recognize everyone that I encountered while on my travels: the clients who shared their insights, the hardworking staff, gracious local hosts, drivers, translators, and everyone who gave me the gifts of their time, talent, and stories. This book would not exist without you. To say thank you seems inadequate.

For the amazing team at Greenleaf Book Group and River Grove Books, I felt you saw my vision of the book from the start and collaborated in helping it come to life. To the trio of editors, Anne Sanow, Sue Reynard, and Simha Stubblefield, I am grateful for your patience and careful guidance with the manuscript. It has been a joy working with each of you.

There's an old cliché that writing a book is a lonely exercise, but I have found the opposite to be true. I have found communities of writers who were warm and supportive and who understood the hurdles I had to face to extract the essence of my story. I am particularly appreciative of the Oxford Writing Circle, where dozens of members encouraged me by reading excerpts of early drafts and offering guidance for improvement. To those starting out on their own writer's journey, I can't emphasize enough how important this kind of feedback is. Thanks to the magical London Writers' Salon. The community that you've nurtured has been essential to this book. From agonizing over the first manuscript, where large portions were written during the early morning at the Writers' Hour sessions, to sharing bits and pieces at Open Mic nights, I have felt the warm embrace of the community through my work on this project.

I am indebted to the many people who read early versions of the work and offered feedback and suggestions: Jonathan Miles, Jan Long Harris, Abbey Vint, Tiffany Williams, Sarah Milne Das, Kevin Elliott, John O'Neill, Lucy Perkins, Catherina Celosse, Sofia Koutlaki, Jo Blackshaw, Maz Green, Maria Carson, Kathryn Koromilas, and additional members of OWC and LWS. Without your constructive and actionable input and cheerleading, I would have probably stopped a long time ago.

To all the family members, friends, colleagues, and associates who have patiently encouraged my effort over these many months, I am humbled by your kindness. And finally, thanks to my husband, Eric Drexler, for his unwavering support and inspiration, without which none of this would have been written.